Action stations
CORAL
SEA

The Australian
Commander's Story

Chris Coulthard-Clark

Action stations
CORAL
SEA

The Australian Commander's Story

ALLEN & UNWIN

Title page photographs: AWM neg. 792, IWM neg. 56165, HU 56166

First published 1991
Allen & Unwin Australia Pty Ltd
8 Napier Street, North Sydney NSW 2059 Australia

National Library of Australia
Cataloguing-in-Publication entry:
Coulthard-Clark, C. D. (Christopher David), 1951–
    Action stations Coral Sea: the Australian
    commander's story.

    Bibliography.
    Includes index.
    ISBN 0 04 442251 2.

    1. Crace, Sir John Gregory. 2. Coral Sea, Battle
    of the, 1942. 3. World War, 1939–1945 — Australia.
    I. Title.

940.5426

Library of Congress Catalog Card Number: 90-055 388

Set in 10.5/12.5 Palatino by SRM Production Services Sdn Bhd, Malaysia
Printed by Kim Hup Lee Printing, Singapore

For my wife Tina
and children
David, Andrew, Gillian and Alyce

Contents

Illustrations

Maps

Acknowledgements

The research for this book was greatly advanced by the interest and assistance of members of the Crace family, namely Reverend Allan Crace and Mr Nicholas Crace (sons of Sir John), Mrs Frena Humphries, and Mr John Crace. Their courtesy in responding to my letters and phone calls, and readiness to make available material in their possession, was a constant encouragement in the project. In particular I should like to express my thanks to the special lengths gone to by Reverend Crace, who looked through his father's papers in the Imperial War Museum on my behalf and thereby greatly facilitated my own use of this source during a brief and busy visit to England in June 1989 while researching a different book. The hospitality extended by Reverend Crace and his wife Rosemary during a weekend visit to their home was also very much appreciated, and it was a pleasure to be able to reciprocate during their subsequent holiday in Australia in October.

I also express my appreciation for the assistance readily given by many participants in the Coral Sea battle, both Australian and American. Special thanks are due to Mrs Mary Kramer of Youngstown, Ohio, who as Honorary Secretary of the USS *Chicago* Reunion Committee provided material and — no less importantly — put me in touch with members of *Chicago*'s crew living in the US, among them Mr Frank Timmerman, Mr Frank Westley and Mr Ed Znosko. These gentlemen all have my sincere thanks for the personal recollections and photographs they contributed. I am no less grateful to those officers and men of HMAS *Australia* and HMAS *Hobart* who responded to my appeals for help by recounting events, loaning photographs, and in some cases reading draft sections of manuscript to give helpfully critical comments. These men included Vice-Admiral Sir Richard Peek, Commodore Allen Dollard, Commodore Dacre Smyth, Captain Charles Savage, Lieutenant-

Commander Roger Moag, Mr Roy Scrivener, Mr Cliff Hemming, Mr Mervyn Johnston and Mr Jack Langrell. My thanks, too, to Mrs Jean Farncomb, widow of Rear-Admiral Harold Farncomb, for her patient response to my inquiries and for putting me in touch with Mr Alan Zammit. Alan's broad range of contacts proved of inestimable value in reaching those former crew members of the two Australian cruisers I have already mentioned, and I am in his debt for the extra lengths to which he went on my behalf to ensure I received the sort of information I was seeking.

In the course of my research, many other individuals and organisations gave me access to material or the benefit of their special knowledge. Here I should like to say 'Thank you' to the following: Commodore Ian Burnside; Mrs Helen Digan (Canberra and District Historical Society); Mr Lyall Gillespie; Rear-Admiral Bill Graham; Lieutenant Keith McCarron (Navy Photographic Unit); Mr John Partridge (records manager, NSW Department of Corrective Services); Mr Rick Pelvin (Historical Officer, Navy Office, Canberra); Mr Jon Wickham (Headmaster, The King's School); Mr Peter Yeend (Archivist, The King's School); and the staffs of the National Library of Australia, the Victorian regional office of Australian Archives, the Imperial War Museum, London, and the Australian War Memorial.

Final thanks go to Mr John Iremonger of Allen & Unwin, whose contribution to shaping this work went—I am sure—beyond what most publishers would be prepared to undertake, and to my family who heroically put up with the disruption and inconvenience that invariably occurs with every book I write.

Abbreviations

AB	Able Seaman
ACH	Area Combined Headquarters
Adel	Adelaide
AWM	Australian War Memorial, Canberra
Canb	Canberra
CNS	Chief of the Naval Staff
COMANZAC	Commander, Anzac Force
COMSOUWESPAC	Commander, South West Pacific Forces
Eng	England
Hants	Hampshire, England
HMAS	His Majesty's Australian Ship
HMS	His Majesty's Ship
HMSO	Her Majesty's Stationery Office
HMNZS	His Majesty's New Zealand Ship
IWM	Imperial War Museum, London
Lond	London
Melb	Melbourne
NHSA	Naval Historical Society of Australia
NLA	National Library of Australia, Canberra
NSW	New South Wales
OD	Ordinary Seaman
RAAF	Royal Australian Air Force
RACAS	Rear-Admiral Commanding, Australian Squadron
RAN	Royal Australian Navy
RN	Royal Navy
SWPA	South West Pacific Area
TKS	The King's School, Parramatta
USS	United States Ship

Introduction

The Battle of the Coral Sea, a series of disjointed and often highly confused naval actions fought off Australia's north-eastern coast on 4–8 May 1942, has long held a special place in the annals of warfare at sea. As a battle carried on principally by American and Japanese squadrons of carrier-borne aircraft, it was the first naval engagement in history in which the opposing forces of surface ships involved at no stage sighted or directly engaged each other.

More than this, it represented the first occasion on which Japanese naval forces, enjoying an unbroken run of successes since the start of the Pacific War in December 1941, experienced the failure of a major operation. The massed-carrier action fought in mid-Pacific off Midway Island a month later was to prove strategically more decisive, entailing losses by Japan which effectively ended that country's hopes of establishing total dominance over US naval strength in the Pacific, but this in no way diminishes the fact that it was at the Coral Sea that Japanese ambitions were first blunted, and the foundations for the Midway victory laid.

At the time that the Coral Sea battle took place, however, it held a sharper and more immediate significance for Australians, many of whom believed that it had turned the tide at a point in the Pacific War when their nation stood in gravest peril. The Coral Sea was hailed as a US Navy victory which forestalled an imminent Japanese invasion of Australia.

The latter view of the battle's significance was wrong on two crucial counts. In the first place, the Japanese operation which precipitated the clash was directed at seizing the major Allied base at Port Moresby. It had no object involving actual invasion of the Australian mainland, nor—as was confirmed after the war—was it a preliminary move towards such an operation. Interviewed shortly before he was hanged as a war criminal in 1948, Japan's wartime prime minister, General Hideki Tojo, denied that invasion of Australia had ever been planned, claiming: 'We never had enough troops to do so . . . We expected to occupy all New Guinea, to maintain Rabaul as a holding base, and to raid northern Australia by air. But actual physical invasion — no, at no time.'

Notwithstanding such disclaimers, the belief that the Coral Sea engagement had been Australia's salvation retained a powerful hold over the popular imagination after the war, receiving potent reinforcement from time to time. Foremost among those who promoted the myth was Australian writer George Johnston, probably best known as author of the novel *My Brother Jack* (1964). During the Pacific War, Johnston had been an official war correspondent accredited to the Australian Army and the RAAF, the US Army, and for a time the RAN. His syndicated despatches to the home front brought the fighting vividly before Australians and earned him a national reputation.

Faced with the post-war necessity of making a living by his pen, Johnston produced some blatantly commercial articles, including one on the Coral Sea appearing in *Australasian Post* on 9 May 1946 under the title 'Battle that saved Australia'. Here he cited the claim allegedly made to him in Japan the previous year by Vice-Admiral Paul Wenneker, the German naval attaché in Tokyo throughout the war, that the Coral Sea battle had completely upset a Japanese masterplan for Pacific conquest which envisaged the conquest of Australia by January 1943. In a highly coloured description of the battle itself, Johnston maintained that the object of the Japanese operation had indeed been 'to soften up Australia for the subsequent continental conquest'. Against this sort of journalism, the true facts of the matter were slow to gain acceptance.

Added to the misconception of the Coral Sea as the battle which 'saved' Australia, there is usually a notion that the US Navy alone did the saving. There can be no denying that the force which frustrated the Japanese plan in May 1942 was commanded by an American admiral, or that the majority of the ships under this officer's command — including the two aircraft carriers which were the principal combat units — were US Navy vessels; but this force was truly an *Allied* one. Not only were major units of Australia's navy participants in the battle, but portion of the Allied fleet — including US vessels as well as the Australian ships — was under the command of the senior seagoing commander serving with the Royal Australian Navy, Rear-Admiral J. G. Crace.

Somewhat ironically, during his days as war correspondent Johnston expressed irritation at American attempts to promote an idea that the US had 'saved' Australia single-handed. As his most recent biographer points out, Johnston complained in his notebooks about American attempts to denigrate or conceal the extent of Australia's burden, and belittle Australian successes, in the campaign fought in New Guinea later in 1942.

But Johnston himself did much to promote the same misleading view. For example, in his 1943 book *New Guinea Diary* (published in the US under the title *The Toughest Fighting in the World*), he provided a relatively restrained and (within the sources then available) reasonably accurate account of the Coral Sea. This, however, recorded his belief that the battle was an action which changed the whole situation affecting Australia overnight, for which the greatest credit was due to the US Navy. In *Pacific Partner* (1944) he summed up the Coral Sea action with the declaration: 'The Battle for New Guinea had been staved off by the skill and courage of the United States Navy, which had chalked up its first triumph over Japan in the long struggle to avenge Pearl Harbor'. When it came to writing his later *Post* article, Johnston did at least acknowledge the involvement of Australian ships, though it was in a single paragraph at the end.

Though subsequent books and articles have given rather better treatment to the facts of RAN participation at the Coral Sea, up till now no attempt has been made to look at the battle through Australian eyes. This study attempts to do that by telling the story primarily of Rear-Admiral Crace, the only Australian commander with a significant role to play in what is still the largest naval clash to have occurred in proximity to Australia. The fact that Crace was actually an officer of the Royal Navy, not the RAN, scarcely matters here, for—as this book also shows—his personal origins and background entitle him to be regarded as an Australian. Above all else, this book is a tribute to the men who found their place in history as participants in a desperate conflict, at sea and in the air, during those first days of May nearly fifty years ago—Australian, American and Japanese.

1 *Australian luck*

I T was shortly after 4 o'clock on Saturday afternoon, 16 September 1939. Jack Crace had just come in from scything the orchard which covered the bottom quarter of the two-acre garden of Hawkley House, his home in the Hampshire countryside. Normally he employed a man (a retired Royal Navy stoker petty officer) to maintain the grounds of the former vicarage of the village of Hawkley, a half-hour train ride from the southern English naval base at Portsmouth, where he and his wife had lived for the past three years. But with the Second World War now less than a fortnight old, their gardener had been called up for naval duty again and Crace was obliged to be his own groundsman.

The telephone rang, and Crace was soon in conversation with a caller from the Admiralty in London. He had been expecting this call for weeks, ever since his promotion from captain to rear-admiral on 1 August. For the last two-and-a-half years he had held a post on the Admiralty staff as assistant to the Second Sea Lord, the arcane title of the chief of naval personnel. As head of the Office for Appointments, he had been responsible for the appointments of all officers below the rank of captain and arranging the officer manning of ships of the Reserve Fleet in the event of war. This was not a job Crace enjoyed. As he later recounted, it all too frequently seemed that there were only square pegs — and too few of them — to fill the many round holes, and he was often compelled to adopt the advice of a colleague who counselled that any shaped peg would fit any shaped hole provided one hit it hard enough. Following his promotion to flag rank he was relieved of his Admiralty job and had been waiting at home for word of the duties to which he was being assigned.

The voice on the other end of the line gave him the news he had been dwelling on, and he could scarcely believe his luck. He had

1

been selected to become 'Rear-Admiral Commanding, Australian Squadron', or RACAS as the post was known in service shorthand. The two-year term of the RN officer filling the post, Rear-Admiral Wilfred Custance, would ordinarily have had some seven months still to run, but Custance had been forced through the sudden onset of a fatal illness to vacate the job the day before the declaration of war in Europe, and the Australian government, following established practice, looked to the Admiralty to supply a successor. Crace pulled out his trunks and began packing that afternoon, but it was a week before he boarded the passenger liner *Orontes* and sailed for Australia to take up the appointment.

For John Gregory Crace, the choice of his appointment was a double pleasure. In the first place, it was a seagoing command — the wish of any newly appointed flag officer, even though the Royal Australian Navy was small (so small, in fact, that from August 1926 it had ceased to be referred to as a fleet and was termed a squadron only). Additionally, his new job meant Crace was returning to the land of his birth.

Crace was born fifty-two years earlier into a family formerly prominent in the Queanbeyan district of New South Wales. In 1880 his father, Edward Kendall Crace, scion of a wealthy and well-connected London family of interior decorators, had established himself as the local squire by acquiring three pastoral stations known as Gungahleen, Ginninderra and Charnwood. On the first of these, Edward Crace extended and remodelled the existing station homestead to provide a large and stylish residence for his family, which ultimately numbered nine children — two sons and seven daughters. In 1883 a two-storey sandstone wing in the popular late Victorian style was built, overlooking a carriage loop and garden planted with English trees and shrubs, a dam forming a miniature lake, and a driveway, again lined with exotic trees. Here the family lived in considerable comfort, even purportedly surrounded by Indian servants for a time.

Young Jack Crace had been raised on the Gungahleen estate, apart from a period of nearly two years (in 1890–92) when the whole family made an extended visit overseas to give the elder children the benefit of an English education. His parents had just returned to Gungahleen with Jack and two of his sisters, leaving the other children with relatives in England, when the family suffered severe financial losses during the Australian banking crisis of March–April 1892. Worse misfortune followed with the death of

Above A childhood photograph an admiral might prefer to forget: taken around 1890, Jack Crace is shown aged about three (in centre, on rocking horse) with his sisters (clockwise from rear) Clara, Dorothy, Bessie, Ursula and Ethel. (*Humphries collection, NLA*) *Below* The south face of Gungahleen mansion in the 1890s, showing the Victorian-style extension at left of the original Georgian homestead. (*Mr E. J. L. Crace*)

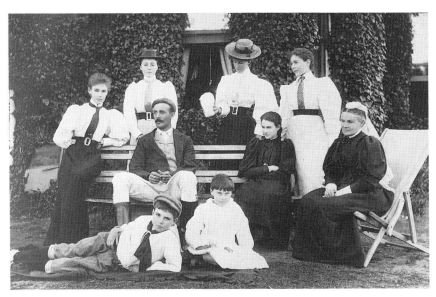

Above The Crace family pose outside the ivy-covered house at Gungahleen around 1897. Jack is reclining on the grass, with Sylvia seated beside him. Everard sits on the bench flanked by Ursula (right) and Clara (left). The girls standing are (from left) Dorothy, Ethel (with cockatoo on her hand) and Bessie. Mrs Kate Crace is seated in the folding chair at right. (*Rev. J. A. Crace*) *Below* The King's School at Parramatta, about the time Crace entered as a boarder in 1898. Many of the students are wearing the uniform of the school cadet corps which was redolent of the American civil war. (*Rev. J. A. Crace*)

Edward Crace in a drowning accident in September of the same year. Jack was only five when he lost his father, and his elder brother Everard, then aged eighteen and working for a London wool business, was recalled from England to help their mother manage the heavily mortgaged estate.

In these less affluent circumstances, Jack Crace continued his childhood at Gungahleen before commencing his formal education in Sydney. After attending a preparatory school, he entered The King's School — Australia's oldest, established at Parramatta in 1832 to remove the need to send boys to England for an education. As a boarder he was a member of the school cadet corps, learning small-arms drill with Martini rifles fitted with bayonets so big for the boys that Crace, by then aged twelve, recalled his used to drag along the ground. After a year at the school, he left in September 1899. The next month he embarked for England to prepare himself for a career in the Royal Navy.

What motivated him towards this choice of career Crace could never explain. He freely admitted that he had rarely even seen the sea, and knew nothing of the navy or the lifestyle entailed in this service. Nonetheless, it had been his ambition from his earliest days, a fact attested to by his usual appearance in a sailor suit in photographs of the family at Gungahleen. Under the guardianship of an uncle living at Portman Square, near London's Hyde Park, he spent a year at a private school before enrolling in 1901 at Foster's Academy at Stubbington. This establishment specialised in preparing boys to meet the educational levels required for entry to the navy.

The training establishment for officers for the Royal Navy at this time was HMS *Britannia*, a wooden vessel moored permanently with HMS *Hindustan* in the estuary of the river Dart in Devon, about a mile from the mouth, as a stationary school for naval cadets. Normally admission to the training ship entailed passing a competitive entrance examination, but in fact Crace was not faced with the same requirements as other candidates for selection. As an Australian he was eligible for a reserved vacancy known as a colonial cadetship, and he was only required to achieve sufficient marks to qualify. By this means he joined the *Britannia* in May 1902 as 76th in an intake of 77 cadets.

A spartan year on board the training ship followed. In a reminiscence written years later, Jack Crace described the facilities on board:

We had no privacy at all and all our possessions were stowed in a sea chest separated from the next one by about a foot; these chests were ranged in rows back to back about six feet apart and in that alleyway we had to dress. At night hammocks were slung above our chests and in these we slept. Our bathing arrangements were also rather primitive and consisted of large tanks containing cold salt water about two feet deep some way from our hammocks. In winter the run to and from the bath and the plunge into icy water was not enjoyable but doubtless helped to harden us up. In winter too the ships were very draughty as the squareports (or windows) were so thick with paint that they could not shut properly and the decks were always wet and very slippery.

Apart from the lack of physical comforts, the discipline was also a new experience. Writing to his mother a few days after his arrival, he reported that 'news' (new cadets) had to do everything at the double and were made to go aloft to sing songs. He reported that one new boy who punched a tormentor from the senior class was to receive a caning from cadets of that class using the stretch-rod from a hammock.

The training was nonetheless invaluable preparation for a life at sea, combining theoretical subjects like navigation and astronomy with plenty of practical seamanship. Crace later recalled that among the staff at this time was William Napier, then a junior officer but later a rear-admiral who became Chief of the Naval Staff and First Naval Member of the Australian Naval Board in 1926–29. The year in *Britannia* was followed by a three-month training cruise in Scottish waters aboard HMS *Isis* and HMS *Aurora*, and then final examinations. Crace graduated 47th in his course at a prize-giving ceremony at Keyham Barracks, Devonport, in September 1903.

Crace was sent to the armoured cruiser *Good Hope*, the flagship of the Cruiser Squadron in the Channel Fleet, initially still as a naval cadet but after a month becoming a midshipman. The *Good Hope* was his home for the next three years and he did well in this ship, being judged in his captain's reports as a smart, reliable, zealous and capable young officer of great promise. In 1906 his captain, writing to a naval friend in Sydney, Vice-Admiral Sir Wilmot Fawkes (commander-in-chief of the Australian Station), mentioned

---

Moored at Dartmouth, HMS *Britannia* and HMS *Hindustan* served as the Royal Navy's officer training establishment. Crace was a naval cadet here from May 1902 until graduating in September 1903. (*IWM neg.HU56175*)

Jack Crace as a midshipman in the Royal Navy. He never could
remember what prompted him to embark on a naval career. (*Rev. J. A.
Crace*)

that Crace was now his assistant and praised the midshipman's diligence and hard work — compliments which were duly conveyed by Fawkes to Crace's mother.

Promoted sub-lieutenant at the end of 1906, by early 1907 Crace was engaged in studies ashore at Portsmouth, followed later in that year by advanced training in theoretical subjects at the Royal Naval College at Greenwich. Not until April 1908 was he back with a ship, this time the protected cruiser HMS *Powerful*, the flagship of the British squadron operating in Australian waters. Once more, it seemed, being born in Australia had stood him in good stead.

This appointment was very congenial, because in Crace's words he found life on the Australian Station to be 'pretty easy'. He much enjoyed the long cruises which took in the main cities of Australia, New Zealand and Fiji, and the summer visits to Hobart for the annual regatta and races which the admiral usually attended with his wife and staff. Being based at Sydney also allowed him to see something of his family and home after an absence of nine years. His mother and several unmarried sisters still lived in the ivy-covered mansion at Gungahleen, with his brother Everard as manager of the property. After about eighteen months on the Australian coast, including several months in HMS *Pyramus*, one of the small cruisers of the local squadron, Crace returned to England. He had been promoted lieutenant in September 1908 while still in the *Powerful*.

From March 1910 his new berth was aboard HMS *Inflexible*, a new armoured cruiser serving with the Home Fleet which Crace recalled as his most unhappy ship. Later in the year he received his first command — *T.B.105*, a torpedo boat serving as a tender to HMS *Defiance*, the vessel housing the Torpedo School afloat at Devonport. Less than a year later, in mid-1911, he was sent to HMS *Vernon*, the Torpedo School establishment at Portsmouth. Here he underwent specialist training as a torpedo officer, covering the operation and maintenance of torpedoes as well as a ship's complete electrical system (including lighting, power for machinery and the gun turrets, telephones and other communications equipment) which formed part of that officer's duties at sea. Here he acquired the nickname 'Crack' Crace, which stayed with him.

From Portsmouth it was off to the Nore in September 1912 for duty with the Second Fleet as Torpedo Lieutenant in the battleship HMS *Formidable*. This was not seagoing, however, as the *Formidable* had been reduced to a nucleus crew earlier that year. Fortunately

for Crace this appointment was not a prolonged one, and early the next year he found himself on loan from the Admiralty for duty with the Australian government and once more back in his country of birth.

The Australian government had decided to establish a seagoing navy and was in the process of acquiring a force of light cruisers and destroyers, along with submarines, which would be capable of independent operation in Australian waters but would come under Admiralty control in time of war. The flagship of this local fleet would be a 19 200-ton battle-cruiser called HMAS *Australia*. Crace joined this vessel, then still building in a Clyde shipyard, in January 1913 as torpedo officer. As he later said, he had once more profited by his Australian origin. Although it was intended that the ships of the Australian Fleet would be manned as far as possible by Australians, this still necessitated the initial loan of some 850 British personnel to what became known from October 1911 as the Royal Australian Navy. Commissioned in June 1913, the *Australia* was at the head of six other warships when the Australian Fleet made its grand entrance into Sydney Harbour on a fine spring morning four months later.

Crace's job as Torpedo Lieutenant while the ship was under construction entailed more than just a responsibility for the torpedo armament being installed, including also the complete electrical equipment. It was a measure of his professional pride and dedication to his work that he took the initiative in compiling an 'Electrical Detail Book for H.M.A.S. Australia'. When this manual came to the authorities' attention late in 1913 he was paid an allowance for the expenses incurred and commended by the Naval Board in Melbourne for 'the zeal displayed . . . in the preparation of the book'.

With the ship's completion and arrival in Australia, Crace continued to think up new ways of improving its operation. Early in 1914 it was revealed that he and Lieutenant Alec Doyle RAN, the

---

The British squadron in Australian waters pictured in Sydney Harbour for an unknown special occasion. At left is HMS *Powerful*, on which Crace served from 1908–10. When built in 1895 *Powerful* and her sistership *Terrible* were the largest protected cruisers afloat, but they were soon superseded by armoured ships and by 1905 *Powerful* was relegated to being flagship on the distant Australian Station. (*IWM neg.HU56177*)

Pictured here in Sydney Harbour is HMAS *Australia*, flagship of the Royal Australian Navy, following its arrival from England in October 1913. Crace was Torpedo Lieutenant aboard the battle-cruiser from the time it was still under construction until 1917. (*RAN Photographic Unit*)

ship's engineer officer, had invented 'a contrivance for the control etc. of searchlights'. Estimates were made of the cost of fitting the device to the *Australia*, and the Naval Board again expressed appreciation of the 'zeal and ingenuity' displayed by the two officers, adding that London would be informed. In the event the Admiralty judged that the invention, although very clever, was too elaborate and costly for service purposes and decided against adopting it, but this did not detract from the initial achievement and nor did it discourage Crace.

During his second posting in Australian waters, Crace found great changes taking place around his birthplace, following the selection of the surrounding district as the site of the new national capital, Canberra. In January 1911 the Commonwealth had taken possession of its federal territory, and the process of resuming land in private hands had begun. At the time of his return, Crace's mother remained in residence at Gungahleen with three of his sisters. Two other sisters had recently married — Ursula in December 1911 to the son of Sir Edmund Barton, first prime minister of Australia and then still serving as Senior Puisne Judge of the High Court, and Clara in April 1912 to Captain Richard Waller of the British Army, then serving as instructor of military engineering at the Royal Military College opened the previous year at the nearby Duntroon property which the Commonwealth had already resumed.

Continued possession of the family home was obviously of uncertain duration. Eventually, in 1915, Crace's mother went to live at Double Bay in Sydney. Her unmarried daughters went with her, the youngest, Sylvia, eventually marrying in April 1917 the son of Canon A. H. Champion (the rector of St John's Church, Canberra, 1909–13, and the headmaster of The King's School while Jack Crace had been a student there).* Everard obtained a lease of part of Gungahleen, including the homestead, and took up residence with his family.

By the time the Commonwealth actually resumed the family property, Jack Crace was gone from Australia again. The First World War had begun in August 1914 and he was now on active service with the Royal Australian Navy's flagship. For several months the *Australia* was engaged in trying to trap two fast cruisers which formed the main battle units of the German East Asia Squadron in the Pacific. After these were destroyed by other British warships in an action off the Falkland Islands in December, the *Australia* was sent to join the Grand Fleet in British home waters. Arriving at Plymouth on 28 January 1915, it became the flagship of the Second Battle Cruiser Squadron based at Rosyth, Scotland, the following month.

Never at more than four hours notice to sail, *Australia* was now constantly involved in sweeps of the North Sea, undertaken in the hope of meeting up with elements of the German High Seas Fleet. There were no fleet engagements, however, the only such clash having taken place at Dogger Bank four days before *Australia* reached England. The one opportunity to take part in a major sea

---

* Arthur Champion, the Canon's son, had also been a student at The King's School (1897–1902). On his death in 1961, a bequest in his will established the Crace-Champion Scholarship at the school, commemorating himself and his brother-in-law, Admiral Sir John Crace. Awarded for the first time in 1972, the scholarship subsequently has been awarded in 1976, 1980, 1983 and 1989.

action — in fact the biggest naval clash of the war — was denied to Crace and everyone else aboard *Australia*. While the squadron was making a sweep on 22 April 1916, in line abreast formation and zigzagging at 19 knots, a dense fog suddenly came down, in which the Australian flagship collided with its sister ship HMS *New Zealand*. The *Australia* sustained damage which required it to undergo repairs at Devonport dockyard for more than a month, and the ship was actually on its way to rejoin the Fleet when the Battle of Jutland was fought on 31 May.

Probably to relieve some of the frustration and tedium associated with sea duty on this basis, Crace continued to apply his mind to solving technical problems. In mid-1915 he had invented a torpedo safe range indicator, at about the same time that an officer in HMS *Lion* produced a similar device. The Admiralty approved the manufacture of six of each type of device for trials, adding that it considered much credit was due to both men 'for the great skill shewn [sic] in the production of these instruments'. The following year, Crace and another officer of the *Australia*, Lieutenant Hugh Vaughan-Williams, collaborated in producing a 'Book of Questions in Torpedo' as a guide for midshipmen preparing themselves for the examination for promotion to lieutenant rank. The outcome of their efforts was that the Admiralty decided to take over the book as an official publication, having copies printed and circulated throughout the navy's ships. Again, the authors were commended for 'the care and trouble taken by them in the compilation of this useful manual'.

Crace's stint at sea came to an end early in 1917. Having been promoted lieutenant-commander the previous September, he was now sent as an instructor to the mining school at Portsmouth. His departure from *Australia* was very much the RAN's loss, with his former captain describing him as 'a most excellent Lieut T [Torpedo Lieutenant] full of ability and resource and never at a loss when carrying out repairs or introducing improvements'. When he left the ship the Australian Naval Board asked that the Admiralty convey to Crace an expression of appreciation for his services while on loan, this request being passed to the Commander-in-Chief at Portsmouth in May. Just over eighteen months at the mining school saw him posted back to a ship, but not immediately for sea duty.

In 1915 the Admiralty had gained approval for the construction of four super battle-cruisers to counter capital ships the German Navy was known to be building. When it was learnt that the Germans had suspended work on their vessels, work on three of the British ships was halted in 1917 (they were later dismantled). Work on the fourth, HMS *Hood*, was continued, however. It was launched in August 1918 at the same Glasgow shipyard in which HMAS *Australia* had been built. Displacing 41 200 tons and mounting main armament of eight 15-inch guns, along with twelve 5.5-inch secondary guns, the *Hood* was at that time the largest and most powerful warship afloat.

Crace was sent to the giant *Hood* as torpedo officer in October 1918. The ship was designed to carry six 21-inch torpedo tubes, two submerged and four above the waterline, and his job was involved with the installation of these and the ship's electrical gear while fitting-out was still under way. During this period he had met Carola Baird, the daughter of a Glasgow lawyer. The ship was finally completed in March 1920 and he married Carola Baird the next month. Then it was off to sea; after commissioning on 15 May, *Hood* joined ten other British warships on a summer cruise to Scandinavia, at the conclusion of which it returned to Scapa Flow.

At the end of 1920 Crace was promoted commander and left the *Hood* for a desk job at the Admiralty. From January 1921 he was on the naval staff in the department of the Director of Torpedoes and Mining. After another two years it was back to the sea again, this time as executive officer of HMS *Danae*, a 4650-ton cruiser with the First Light Cruiser Squadron. While with this ship, Crace was involved in a particularly remarkable naval episode — one which brought him back to Australian waters. Following Foreign Office consultations with dominion and colonial governments in 1922, a decision was made to send a 'Special Service Squadron' around the world to show the flag and demonstrate the Royal Navy's mastery of the seas. As the largest symbol of British sea power it was natural that *Hood* would lead this world cruise; accompanying it would be the battle-cruiser *Repulse* and the five D class cruisers of the First Light Cruiser Squadron, including *Danae*.

Departing England in November 1923, the British ships travelled down the west coast of Africa and called at several South African ports before heading to the Malay States and Singapore, the proposed site of a naval base to serve as a bastion of the British Empire in South-East Asia. From here the squadron steamed down the Indian Ocean to Australia, making its first call at Fremantle on 28 February. Calls at Albany, Adelaide, Melbourne, Hobart, Jervis Bay, Sydney and Brisbane followed.

15

The Australian portion of the cruise was described by one writer as 'a triumphal procession', the reception accorded the squadron being 'tumultuous, ecstatic'. At each stop an endless round of functions and attractions was staged in the visitors' honour, creating a mad social whirl which caused the cruise to become — in the minds of some — a 'world booze'. The ships were also opened to public inspection, attracting tens of thousands of sightseers.

For Crace, the time spent at Sydney in April meant most because his wife and two-year-old son had travelled out from England in the liner *Euripides* to be with him during the squadron's call at that port. This allowed Crace to introduce them to his mother, now residing at Woollahra, and other family members living in the Sydney area. Everard also brought his family from Canberra to see them. There was, however, a sad aspect to his time in Sydney, as the squadron's call coincided with the sinking of the pride of the Australian Fleet, HMAS *Australia*, to comply with the terms agreed two years earlier at the Washington disarmament conference.

To reduce the British Empire's quota of capital ships to the limits set by the Washington Treaty, the *Australia* was sent to a watery grave 24 miles due east of Sydney Heads on 12 April 1924, amid displays of emotion from witnesses. Four of the British light cruisers, including the *Danae*, were leaving Sydney for Brisbane as the former flagship was being escorted to its final resting place, and fired a respectful salute before turning northward. What Crace felt on this occasion, watching the once-proud ship on which he had seen his war service going to meet its end, can only be imagined.

At the conclusion of the world cruise in September 1924, Crace left the *Danae*, taking with him a report showing that he had been an exceptionally good executive officer who was strongly recommended for early promotion. No notice was taken of the recommendation at this time, however, and he was sent to be the commander of HMS *Osprey*, the newly-formed Anti-submarine School at Portland, Dorset, which came under the control of the captain commanding HMS *Vernon*. Here again he shone for his organising, administrative and technical abilities. Reports raised on him referred to him as an officer 'of outstanding ability, who has consistently displayed zeal, sound judgement and tact of a high order', it also being remarked that he had 'set an example of personal service, consideration & forethought, which must prove of the greatest benefit to all who have served under him'.

Again he had been strongly recommended for early promotion

but instead, a short period of refresher training at the Torpedo School at Portsmouth followed in late 1926, preparatory to his joining next year the staff of Admiral Sir Roger Keyes, Commander-in-Chief of the Mediterranean Station, as Fleet Torpedo Officer. Finally promoted captain in June 1928, the following April Crace was sent to the Atlantic Fleet in command of the destroyer HMS *Valhalla*, the leader of the 6th Flotilla. A year later it was back to commanding the Anti-submarine School, which had so expanded in importance and size that it was now a separate command under a captain. After two years at *Osprey*, in May 1932 he rejoined the naval staff at the Admiralty, this time as Director of the Tactical Division.

Another two years and Crace was back at sea once more, this time as captain of HMS *Emerald*, a cruiser then fitting out to join the 4th Cruiser Squadron on the East Indies Station. He later held this appointment to have been his most enjoyable. The station encompassed the Bay of Bengal, the Arabian Sea including the Persian Gulf, and down the east coast of Africa to the southern border of Tanganyika, and took in all the islands between. Based at Trincomalee in Ceylon, the squadron visited nearly all ports in this area, excepting only the Persian Gulf; due to the international crisis caused by the Italo-Abyssinian conflict of 1935–36, the ships were held at Aden in readiness to counter moves by the Italian Navy. In late May 1936 the illness of the commander-in-chief, Vice-Admiral Frank Rose, forced his return to England, leaving Crace in temporary command with the rank of commodore pending the arrival of a successor. On completion of the *Emerald*'s commission early in 1937, it was back to the Admiralty for Crace and the post in which he was still serving on the outbreak of war.

By 1939, it could be said that Crace had already enjoyed a successful and colourful career. He himself considered that he had received more than his share of luck, attributing much of that good fortune to his Australian origins. Unquestionably this was a factor which had several times exercised an important influence over his career, just as it appeared to have done again with his selection to assume command of the Australian Squadron.

2   *A happy augury*

C RACE'S ship reached Melbourne on the night of 29 October 1939. Though the *Orontes* was obliged to observe war precautions, such as strict darkening of the liner every night, the voyage out had been uneventful. The morning after his arrival Crace met with his superior at navy headquarters, Vice-Admiral Sir Ragnar Colvin on loan from the RN, who was the Chief of the Naval Staff and First Naval Member of the Naval Board controlling the administration of the RAN. He was also introduced to other members of the Naval Board, and to the Military and Air boards and the Defence Secretariat. A lunch at Government House followed, hosted by the State governor (Major-General Sir Winston Dugan) but attended also by the Governor-General, Lord Gowrie, after which Crace left for Sydney to take over his new command.

At 9.30am on 1 November, Crace hoisted his flag in HMAS *Canberra*. This was for him an event heavily laden with symbolism, a fact to which he had alluded in a press interview while passing through Melbourne: 'To me the command of the Australian squadron is an extremely interesting job, to which I look forward with unqualified pleasure, both for personal and service reasons.' Addressing the Millions Club in Sydney a fortnight later, he referred even more directly to the link: 'Speaking as an Australian, I feel highly honoured to be chosen to command our Navy, and it is a happy augury that my flag flies from a ship named after my home town, Canberra.'

The press was also alert to Crace's Australian connection, the Melbourne *Argus* reporting that he was the first Australian to hold the position as the RAN's seagoing commander. The claim that he was the first local appointee was actually wrong; as the Melbourne *Age* more correctly noted, two of his fifteen predecessors—J. S. Dumaresq (commanding in 1919–22) and R. C.

Dalglish (1932–34) — had been Australian-born RN officers like himself, and one — G. F. Hyde (1926–29) — was an English-born officer of the RN who transferred to the RAN in 1912. Nonetheless, the emphasis of press reports remained firmly on Crace's Australianness. Under the headline 'An Australian Admiral', the *Sydney Morning Herald* declared: 'As an Australian, Rear-Admiral J. G. Crace will be assured of a special welcome from the Royal Australian Naval Squadron, to whose command he has just been appointed.'

This might have seemed to be rather stretching a point. Crace was not, after all, a member of the local forces but an expatriate. Apart from his two pre-First World War postings to ships serving on the Australian Station, and a later transit of Australian ports, he had not been resident for forty years. One might have reasonably expected that in this interval the links forming a tangible Australian identity would have greatly diminished. Certainly his mother was now gone, having died at her Woollahra home in September 1926; with Everard's death in January 1928 the house at Gungahleen had finally passed from family hands.

Yet Crace evidently felt his Australian connections keenly, and retained an ongoing sentimental attachment to his origins. The terms in which he spoke to local journalists revealed the deep nostalgia he felt for his birthplace. Despite the passage of time, he still remembered the Canberra of his childhood — a time, in fact, before Canberra existed. He wistfully recalled the few public buildings which then dotted the Limestone Plains: the Church of St John the Baptist where he was christened, the parsonage, the tiny cottage which also served as post office, the pub and the shoeing forge, and the store. 'You know the sort of store, with a stone bottle of ginger beer in the window. Yes, I knew that stone bottle quite well...'

From the moment of his arrival Crace also enjoyed meeting up with his sisters living in Sydney, and renewed his association with old family friends. Another cherished link that he repaired at this time was with The King's School, where he held the distinction of being the 'leading sailor Old Boy', the first former student to have attained flag officer rank in the navy. He visited the school for speech day in December, and two months later attended the annual dinner of the Old Boys Union.

Crace's local connection was, moreover, very likely a factor in his selection for the post, judging from immediate precedents. Only

19

the previous year London had been requested to provide a replacement for the head of the Royal Australian Air Force, and although the Australian government subsequently settled upon a local appointee for the post, it was probably significant that the British Air Ministry had nominated a Sydney-born air marshal (Sir William Mitchell). Crace's appointment so soon after this instance seems to suggest that British authorities had a definite policy of selecting candidates of local origins for senior dominion posts, presumably on the basis that they would be more acceptable to local sentiment. In view of the reception Crace's appointment received, this judgement was correct.

Indeed, considerable attention was focussed on his arrival. One newspaper, comparing him with his predecessor, declared: 'A more remarkable contrast of naval types than the two rear-admirals it would be hard to imagine, with Custance as the John Bull of the Navy, a fighting heavy-weight, muscled like a gladiator, and Crace as the modern stream-lined naval athlete of the early fifties.' Some six months later, another Sydney journal would remark that his appearance 'might suggest a somewhat ascetic but active bishop' when seen for the first time:

> As a bishop he would certainly be an ornament to the Church Militant, for he has all the detached and human forcefulness of one who has handled men from his short-trouser days and who has been cooped up with hundreds of them long enough to understand them inside out.

It was reported in the *Sydney Morning Herald* that Crace brought with him a message from the First Lord of the Admiralty, Winston Churchill: 'Before he left England he saw the First Lord . . . who told him to tell the Australians to keep their spirits up, because England was full of confidence and there was nothing to fear.' His address to the Millions Club on 13 November was also fully reported in the press, particularly his statement that he had closely investigated all that was being done to strengthen local naval preparedness and he was 'more than satisfied with the result'. He would, he said, like to tell the club of the splendid work that was being done in the equipping and arming of the merchant service for war emergencies, but he 'could not talk about that in these troubled times' apart from saying that the conversion of merchant ships in Sydney was being carried out 'most efficiently'. Applauding the work of volunteers for the various subsidiary naval services, he noted that many of these

Rear-Admiral J. G. Crace, on assuming the appointment as flag officer commanding the Australian Squadron in November 1939. (*Rev. J. A. Crace*)

men had given up good shore jobs to rejoin the navy or the auxiliary services and were doing their jobs 'enthusiastically, capably, and unselfishly'.

At the time that Crace acceded to its command, the RAN was a relatively small but by no means insignificant force, its thirteen combatants including two heavy and four light cruisers, five destroyers and two sloops. The heavy cruisers, *Australia* and *Canberra*, were 10 000-ton County or Kent class ships mounting 8-inch guns. Built in 1928, they were now over ten years old but the *Australia* had just completed a modernisation which included the fitting of increased armour protection. It was due to the presence of *Australia* in the dockyard at the outset of the war that *Canberra*, rather than the national namesake, carried the squadron's commander afloat. While serving as flagship, *Canberra*'s wartime complement of 815 men was bolstered by an additional 30 made up of the admiral and his staff.

The mainstays of the light cruiser force were *Perth*, *Sydney* and *Hobart*, each displacing 7000 tons and mounting 6-inch guns. Originally ordered for the British Admiralty in 1933, these improved Leander class ships had been completed in 1935–36 and represented a modern fighting element. The *Adelaide*, completed in 1922 to a design dating back to 1915–16, was not of the same class but, having been rearmed with 6-inch guns and modernised to counter the increased air and submarine threats, it was still a vessel which commanded respect.

The five ships of the destroyer force—*Stuart*, *Vendetta*, *Waterhen*, *Vampire* and *Voyager*—all dated from 1917–18. Manned by the RAN, they were actually on loan from Britain and strictly speaking remained Admiralty ships. The Sydney-built sloops *Yarra* (1936) and *Swan* (1937), each of 1100 tons and mounting 4-inch guns, were (apart from three boom defence vessels) the only small ships integral to the RAN. Another two sloops of improved design, *Parramatta* and *Warrego*, had been laid down at the Cockatoo Island dockyard at Sydney, but only the *Parramatta* (launched in June 1939) was at an advanced stage to completion.

Apart from these warships, a number of passenger liners had been requisitioned to help bridge the gap until new-construction escort vessels became available. Three such vessels—*Moreton Bay*, *Arawa* and *Kanimbla*—had been impressed after the declaration of war for conversion as armed merchant cruisers. It was undoubtedly to them that Crace had been referring in his address to the Millions

Club, although in October the Naval Board had decided to take over the coastal liners *Manoora* and *Westralia* and convert them to this role as well.

Although an impressive force on paper, Crace soon found that the ships actually available to him did not comprise much of a tactical force. Because the RAN was essentially operating under the Admiralty, as part of the RN, a significant proportion of his strength was not under his control. The *Perth* had yet to be seen in Australian waters; making its passage from England when hostilities began, it had been diverted to the West Indies Station at the Admiralty's request for duty in the Caribbean and western Atlantic areas. The destroyer flotilla was similarly detached, the Australian government having agreed in October to a British request for these vessels to be sent to Singapore (and later to the Mediterranean). Going one further, the War Cabinet had offered a 6-inch cruiser for overseas service too, with the result that *Hobart* had also gone from the squadron Crace had been given to command before he even arrived.

Crace cannot have felt very pleased about his ships being dispersed in this way, but he evidently had nothing to say about the matter at this juncture — later the issue became a major source of friction with the Naval Board. For the present, he set about working up what he had left. The day after his flag was hoisted, he put to sea in the *Canberra*, in company with *Australia* and *Adelaide*, for overnight exercises and patrol. More training followed over the next three weeks, combined with some real work checking out reports of unidentified vessels, as the flagship and *Australia* proceeded down the east coast.

Reaching Melbourne on 20 November, Crace attended a conference at Navy Office to review arrangements made to deal with the appearance of a German raider in the Indian Ocean. Due to the possibility of raiders appearing in the Pacific too, the decision had been made that, until the danger of attack in that quarter was removed, neither of the RAN's heavy cruisers should be released to the Admiralty for service overseas but should be retained to provide for the protection of trade in south-eastern Australian waters. It was also decided to undertake naval patrols on the trade routes across the Indian Ocean where these converged on Fremantle.

Canberra and *Australia* accordingly sailed for Albany on 25 November; arriving on the 28th they began patrolling off Fremantle in company with HMAS *Sydney*. In mounting tedium this patrolling

23

was kept up until 2 December, when news was received that the raider in the Indian Ocean had gone back round the Cape into the Atlantic and was now unlikely to be heading in Australia's direction. *Sydney* headed for Fremantle; *Canberra* and *Australia* proceeded to Albany. After refuelling, the heavy cruisers headed for Sydney via Melbourne, arriving on 8 December, when *Canberra* commenced a minor refit. On completion of this work on 18 December, the flagship and *Australia* went to sea on patrol and for exercises.

After spending Christmas in Sydney, *Canberra* sailed for Wellington on 1 January 1940 to join the convoy being assembled to transport the first New Zealand troops bound for the Middle East. The British battleship *Ramillies* and the New Zealand light cruiser *Leander* were also there, waiting to act as escorts.

Before embarking on the serious business at hand, officers and men from the warships made the most of their time in port, taking in the city's centennial exhibition, including a visit to sideshow alley. The Wellington *Dominion* reported the rollicking good time enjoyed by Crace and his counterpart from the *Ramillies*, observing that in taking to the rides and novelty activities, the two admirals and an accompanying party of dignitaries, including the mayor, 'threw aside dignity to enjoy the main devices':

> The naval officers rode on the cyclone ride and the Jack and Jill, and visited the Crazy House, where they slid down the slide, and tried their sea-legs in the revolving barrel. They broke crockery, tipped the girls out of bed, saw all the sideshows, and raced on the baby cars. Perhaps the highlight of the evening, however, was the spectacle of the commanding officers of the two great warships navigating the little Playland speedboats — and by no means without collisions. They made a hilarious tour of the amusement park, and neglected hardly a sideshow.

Canberra was in the lead when the convoy of six troopships put to sea on 6 January. An uneventful passage of the Tasman saw the convoy reach Sydney two days later to pick up four transports loaded with the first elements of the Second Australian Imperial Force (AIF), also bound for the Middle East. *Canberra* led these ships to a rendezvous with the New Zealand troopships 30 miles off the Heads and at 4 pm the augmented convoy proceeded south. An additional transport was gathered into the fold off Port Phillip Heads on 12 January before a course was steered out into the Bight.

It was very likely to Crace's relief when the flagship anchored outside Fremantle on 19 January, the delivery of the 13 500 Anzac troops having been accomplished without incident. Waiting at Gage Roads were the French heavy cruiser *Suffren* and HMS *Kent* (the lead ship of the County class of heavy cruisers and thus a sister ship to both *Canberra* and *Australia*). The previous month, the Chief of the Naval Staff, Admiral Colvin, who held command responsibility for close maritime defence of Australia and escort of convoys, had advocated using *Canberra, Australia* and *Sydney* to protect this first convoy to the limit of the Australian Station near Cocos Island. The War Cabinet had demurred at depleting the naval forces remaining in Australian waters, and directed that the Admiralty be asked to provide two 8-inch gun cruisers. The *Suffren* and *Kent* were assigned to replace the Australian cruisers on the convoy's next leg to Colombo.

Although relieved of their charges, the Australian cruisers took up patrol of the area off Fremantle while the convoy prepared to sail on 20 January. With the convoy again on its way, Crace headed back east on 30 January, leaving *Australia* at Fremantle. By 9 February the flagship was back in Sydney, having steamed nearly 9000 miles in the period of less than six weeks since its departure. The opportunity was taken for a short rest and it was nearly two weeks before *Canberra* put to sea again. Before Crace could take a break, however, the day after his arrival he had to attend an important ceremony. The new sloop *Warrego* was launched at Cockatoo Island by the wife of Prime Minister Robert Menzies, and at the same time the laying of keels for two new escort vessels was begun by the prime minister and his minister for the navy, Sir Frederick Stewart; one of these vessels was HMAS *Warramunga*, the second of three Tribal class 2000-ton destroyers.

A ceremony of a different kind took place when HMAS *Perth* finally reached Australia at the end of the next month, having been replaced overseas by the *Sydney*. The day after her arrival in Sydney, 1 April, some 1200 men of the naval forces, including men from *Perth*, marched through city streets with the Governor-General, Lord Gowrie, taking the salute on the steps of the Town Hall. Again Crace was on hand to witness the warm public reception given to the *Perth* crew, and with him for this occasion was his wife.

Carola had written in mid-December to say that she had made up her mind to join her husband after Christmas, an action Crace attempted to discourage because of the anticipated movements of his squadron. Nevertheless she arrived by QANTAS flying boat on

25

Crace (left) with Prime Minister Robert Menzies and Vice-Admiral Sir Ragnar Colvin, Chief of the Naval Staff, at Cockatoo Island Dockyard on 10 February 1940. They were attending ceremonies marking the launch of HMAS *Warrego* by Mrs Menzies, and the laying of keels of two new escort vessels by the prime minister and his minister for the navy. (*IWM neg.HU56163*)

21 February. Initially, the intention was for her to stay about six months, so their three sons remained behind. Allan, the eldest, was in any event already making his own way in the Royal Navy as a midshipman aboard HMS *Southampton,* but 14-year-old Christopher and 11-year-old Nicholas were both at boarding schools. Later, after France fell to the German invasion in June and Britain itself seemed in peril, Crace and his wife decided to bring out the two younger boys. The plan to withdraw Christopher from Eton was resisted by one of the masters there, who urged them to reconsider in the boy's best interests, with the result that only Nicholas travelled out, in the company of a cousin. Nick joined his parents in October, and was enrolled as a boarder at Geelong Grammar School, a prestigious Anglican establishment in Victoria.

With his wife on hand, Crace's life assumed a very different pace. They set up residence in a flat in Rushcutters Bay, but in Sydney's wartime rental market frequent moves followed which found them living at various times in apartments at Onslow Avenue (in that part of Darlinghurst now known as Elizabeth Bay, immediately alongside the naval dockyard at Garden Island), at Point Piper, and Fairfax Road in Bellevue Hill. Carola immersed herself with other wives in the work of the Naval War Auxiliary but they still found plenty of time to spend together, both in social functions and other outings.

One activity they undertook after Carola's arrival was a visit to Canberra. Travelling by train to the national capital on Friday 12 April, they spent the next few days taking in the sights of the federal territory with Everard's son, Richard Crace, and his wife Peggy as guides. In the evenings they dined with the Menzies at the Lodge, the Gowries at Government House and the Whiskards at the residence of the British High Commissioner. The highlight of their stay was undoubtedly a sentimental pilgrimage to Gungahleen on Saturday 13 April (their wedding anniversary). As it had recently changed hands*, the old family home was empty and locked up, but Richard Crace gained entry through the back pantry window and let the others in by opening a drawing-room window. Crace was thus able to have a look over the whole house, which he was disappointed to find was in very bad repair. The outside buildings, too, were in a poor state, and the avenue and garden had degenerated into a wilderness, with many trees lost from the carriage circle in front of the house and around the dam. Another moving moment for the admiral came with a visit to the churchyard at St John's where his parents were buried. On Monday he and Carola took the train back to Sydney.

Shortly after this excursion, the squadron prepared to end two months of short sea exercises and firings with another tour of escort duty. On the morning of 24 April *Canberra* and *Australia* proceeded to sea for final exercises, before carrying on to New Zealand. Wellington was reached on 27 April and four transports shepherded across to Sydney, arriving at a rendezvous off the Heads on 5 May

---

* The lease had just been taken over by Mr Ambrose Kitchen from the long-time holder, Dr Frederick Watson, a Sydney radiologist who was also a well-known historian. In 1949 it passed back to the Department of the Interior, which made the house and 46 acres of grounds available to the Canberra University College. Now known as Gungahlin—the name by which it is called on modern maps of Canberra—the property was used as a hall of residence (housing diplomatic cadets mainly) from 1950 until 1953, when the Commonwealth Scientific and Industrial Research Organisation (CSIRO) established the administrative centre of its Division of Wildlife Research there.

where the giant Cunard liner *Queen Mary*, now in use as a troop-ship, was found with *Sydney* as an escort. This convoy was again escorted on a southward passage and across the Bight to Fremantle.

Arriving at Fremantle on 11 May, the convoy was greeted with the news of the German invasion of France, Belgium and Holland. The next day it sailed for Colombo, with the *Canberra* and *Australia* ordered to remain as escorts as far as Cocos Island before returning to Fremantle to refuel. This plan was abruptly changed, however, with the expectation that Italy was about to enter the war. This meant that the Mediterranean would present greatly heightened risks of troopships coming under air and sea attack, and accordingly the convoy was diverted away from the Red Sea. On 16 May, while the convoy was still only halfway to Colombo, new orders were received to proceed via Cape Town, and *Canberra* had to stay with the transports until relieved as escort four days later. Crace immediately set a course for Fremantle, over 3000 miles to the east, and by 5 June the flagship was back in Sydney.

While *Canberra* was berthed at Garden Island for a short refit, Crace learnt that, following consultations between the Australian government and the Admiralty at the end of May, the ship was being sent to serve for a period at the Cape of Good Hope, while *Australia* was required to undertake duties in the Mediterranean or British home waters. As a result, on 7 June Crace transferred his flag from *Canberra* to *Perth* while the two ships were lying alongside at Garden Island.

Protection of troopship movements was an unexciting business, even though most necessary. Until mid-1940 it was essentially precautionary because there had been no known German presence in waters proximate to Australia. On 18 June, however, a liner was sunk by a mine off the north island of New Zealand, revealing that southern Pacific waters were now receiving attention from Axis surface raiders in what was a serious new development. Quite apart from the dangers posed to coastal shipping, periodic transports taking troops abroad now faced a very real threat. A number of enemy ships were obviously operating in areas affecting Australia, because in July merchant ships began disappearing in the Indian Ocean, indicating renewed raider activity on this front at the same time as incidents continued off the coastline of eastern Australia.

As a direct consequence Crace found himself more heavily engaged in troop escort work. Despite the assumed proximity of enemy ships, convoy work continued to be essentially uneventful, with rare moments of excitement having more to do with pretend than real action. One such occasion arose while *Perth* was in the Bight, returning from escorting a westbound troopship, when Crace decided to inspect his flagship at action stations. Checking on the 4-inch gun deck, he gave the order for 'Exercise enemy aircraft approaching Red 40' (that is, to engage a notional air target approaching the port side of the ship at an angle of 40 degrees from the bow). Unfortunately the instructions were given without the knowledge of the Gunnery Officer, Lieutenant Warwick Bracegirdle, so that when the exercise was taken as a real show by a zealous young officer at the mounting there was no-one to prevent the guns being loaded for a live barrage.

Bracegirdle later recalled that, before the Admiral could stop it, six rounds of high explosive on short fuses were fired into the sky, resulting in the destruction of the ship's Supermarine Seagull V amphibian (generally known as a 'Walrus', the name given this aircraft type in the Royal Navy) which was stowed forward of the crane. The aircraft was very susceptible to damage when the guns were fired, and in this case the blast crumpled a wing. According to Bracegirdle: 'The Admiral was naughty as he did not stop the loading and firing and forgot that one should not fire with the aircraft on board, at any rate not on that bearing.'

The destruction in late August of two cargo ships operating between Wellington and Sydney, and the subsequent aerial sighting of a marauder south of the Western Australian port of Albany, provided a renewed sense of purpose for the cruisers performing escort work in Australian waters, including *Canberra*, now back from duty overseas. For two months nothing more was heard from any of the enemy raiders, but at the end of October—while Crace happened to be away with *Perth* in the west—the raider *Pinguin* and her auxiliary laid mines between Sydney and Newcastle, off Hobart, and mined the waters around the Banks Strait, Cape Otway and Wilson's Promontory. Their activities became apparent when the first of two steamers fell victim to the minefields on 7 November, by which time *Pinguin* had headed for the Indian Ocean. Here she sank three ships—*Maimoa*, *Port Brisbane* and *Port Wellington*—before making off into the Antarctic.

The attack on the *Port Brisbane* took place some 800 miles west of Fremantle, and resulted in the *Canberra* immediately racing to the scene on 20 November, followed by *Perth* two days later. Survivors were rescued, but despite an intensive search nothing could be found of the *Pinguin*. The two ships returned to Fremantle on 27 November, and that afternoon Crace transferred his flag from the *Perth* back to the heavy cruiser. Both ships left port the next day as escorts for a convoy bound for Colombo, but on 3 December *Canberra* was relieved and headed back to Fremantle.

En route for that port, a problem developed with a propeller shaft bracket which necessitated docking the ship for repairs at Sydney. Crace did not stay with the *Canberra* as it limped along on this easterly passage. Deciding that it was imperative he visit Navy Office at once to discuss renewed enemy activity off eastern Australia, he flew off on board the ship's Walrus. On the very day that Crace had transferred his flag to *Canberra*, a group of three raiders had revealed their presence by shelling and sinking a passenger ship 500 miles east of Auckland. This attack was followed up the next month by the sinking of five phosphate carriers off the undefended island of Nauru.

There was little that Crace's depleted squadron could do against such tactics; the difficulties of pinning the raiders' locations in vast ocean areas were simply immense, even using air surveillance. On 9 December 1940 the Naval Board advised the Admiralty that they were finding it extremely difficult to meet their commitments with the meagre resources available. In the event, after one of the raiders returned to Nauru to destroy the island's phosphate plant by shellfire on 27 December, no further raider activity took place on the Australian Station for almost a year.

With the passing of the activity associated with the raider menace, Crace began to find his time taken up less and less with duties at sea. After *Canberra* arrived at Sydney on 26 December the cruiser had ceased to be the flagship, and for nearly a month the admiral's flag flew at HMAS *Rushcutter*, a depot on Sydney Harbour. After escorting another convoy from New Zealand late in January 1941, wearing his flag in HMAS *Hobart*, he began experiencing long periods of time in port. Increasingly he began to question the purpose of, and the need for, his presence in Australia.

3 Nothing much doing

B Y the end of 1940 less anxiety was felt in Australia over the situation in home waters than over the growing likelihood of war with Japan. In the words of the *Official History*, 'On the Australian Station the year 1941 was, in the main, a period of building up in preparation for an extension of the war on a major scale in the Far East. Long recognised as a possibility, such extension increasingly loomed as a probability as the year progressed, until the storm finally burst in the Pacific in December.' Illustrating the concern felt within the region, extensive discussion and contingency planning took place throughout 1941 between Australia, New Zealand, Britain, the United States and the Netherlands East Indies regarding the joint measures which might be taken in the event of a Pacific war, and it fell to Crace to play a role in this process.

An Anglo-Dutch-Australian meeting was scheduled to take place at Singapore on 22–25 February to devise a practical and coordinated scheme for reinforcing points in the strategic area in the event of attack. Australia initially planned to send the CNS, Admiral Colvin, with senior officers from the army and air force, to participate in this conference (or what was more loosely termed 'conversations'). On 15 February, however, Australia advised the British Secretary for Dominion Affairs that Colvin would not be able to attend, and that Rear-Admiral Crace would take his place as leader of the Australian and New Zealand delegation. Crace himself learnt of his involvement only two days earlier, when he was told that Colvin would be unable to make the flight to Singapore because he was suffering from high blood pressure and needed rest. Consequently, he left for the conference on the Qantas Empire Airways flying-boat from Sydney's Rose Bay terminal on 18 February.

31

The day after his arrival in Singapore, Crace took part in preliminary discussions with British delegates ostensibly designed to ensure that the British and Australians spoke 'with one voice' in front of the Dutch at the conference itself, where there would also be American observers. He soon found, however, that strong differences of opinion existed. The Commander-in-Chief of the China Station, Vice-Admiral Sir Geoffrey Layton, expressed disagreement with an appreciation by the Australian chiefs of staff of the scope of possible Japanese action, considering it too pessimistic. Crace countered that the movement of a Japanese squadron south into the Tasman Sea was quite plausible, but found his arguments were to no avail.

As the conference proceeded to draft an agreement to provide (subject to government ratification) for mutual assistance in the event of Japanese attack, Crace discovered that differences with Layton persisted. At a sub-committee meeting on naval aspects on the third day, the admiral flatly refused to consider a joint plan to cover 'sea communications' (in this context, the term probably meant protection of trade routes but this is not clear from Crace's diary). Crace tackled him privately about this early the next day, urging the need to include such a plan in the naval portion of the agreement, but found Layton 'would not budge although he was very nice about it'. When the final draft of the agreement was tabled in the conference later that morning, the Australian delegates declared that they wished to go through it before being asked to consider it in a plenary session. When the conference reconvened at 2 pm the final draft was agreed—'as amended by Australians', Crace noted—though still without the naval plan he had sought. The final act of the conference took place at a cocktail party given by the British Commander-in-Chief in the Far East, Air Chief Marshal Sir Robert Brooke-Popham. As Crace recorded, the 'final draft was brought there about 2045 (8.45 pm) and signed!'

With the Singapore negotiations over, Crace headed back to Australia. Arriving in Perth by air on 3 March, he hoisted his flag in the *Hobart* at Fremantle two days later. The next three months were largely taken up with squadron exercises and the escorting of convoys between New Zealand and Australia; the sheer monotony of these activities was probably a factor behind the events which now began to take shape. By early May Crace was recording in his diary problems being experienced with the Naval Board on the matter of operational control of his squadron. He had returned from Singapore to the news that Colvin had resigned as Chief of the Naval Staff because of ill-health and was only awaiting the arrival of his successor. Crace came to believe that the staff at Navy Office were taking decisions which impinged on his role as sea-going commander of the squadron, and demonstrated an unwillingness to take notice of his views.

Within a few weeks the tensions arising over this issue had reached the stage where Crace was beginning to think of his return to the Royal Navy. On 22 May, while the flagship was in port at Melbourne, he called into Navy Office and asked what action had been taken to arrange for his relief when his two-year term as RACAS expired in only five months time. He discovered, however, that Colvin was not anxious for a change, and that the approach being adopted at headquarters was to leave the question of a replacement alone until such time as the Admiralty raised it.

The next day, however, Crace learnt that his Staff Officer (Operations and Intelligence), Lieutenant-Commander George Oldham, had been in a blazing row with an officer named Buchanan at Navy Office.* This member of the headquarters staff accused 'the Flagship' (that is, Crace and his staff) of having taken the opportunity presented by CNS's illness 'to seize power' from the Naval Board but declared that this would be 'soon put right' by the anticipated appearance of Colvin's replacement, Vice-Admiral Sir Guy Royle. Crace hastened to make the two officers patch up this quarrel, but he can hardly have been happy to discover such an attitude in the minds of senior figures of the naval staff.

After receiving a testy letter from the Naval Board regarding the operational control issue, on 9 June Crace wrote privately to Commodore John Durnford RN, then acting CNS, offering to go to Navy Office for discussions aimed at resolving the dispute. Having made all the arrangements to travel by train to Melbourne at the end of the month, he was surprised to receive a short letter from Colvin on 28 June. This stated that he was not prepared to discuss the question of operational control further, but if Crace wished to raise other matters he would be delighted to see him. Crace angrily recorded in his diary that 'it was an extremely rude note and I replied that I had cancelled my berth to Melbourne as I didn't consider my journey would be justified'.

---

* There were two Buchanans on the naval staff — Herbert James and Alfred Edgar — both holding commander rank; which of them had clashed with Oldham is unclear.

In this stand-off situation he was further surprised to see that when the King's Birthday honours were publicly announced a few days later all mention of him having been made a Companion in the Order of the Bath (CB) was omitted from the local press — even though his award was the highest to an Australian naval figure. He recorded that he was 'amused' to see that all other awards in the RAN had been published on 1 July, but there is little reason to doubt that he was peeved by the omission, which he interpreted as a petty slight aimed at him personally by figures at Navy Office. Not until 3 July was his CB reported in the Australian press.

By early July, however, Admiral Royle had arrived and Crace began taking his grievances up with the new chief. On 10 July he asked whether Royle knew anything about his replacement, learning only that an appointment was expected to be made from the batch of officers to be next promoted. Anticipating that his own successor would be named and on the way to Australia within a matter of two months, the very next day he started a letter to the Naval Board proposing a reorganisation of his duties as RACAS 'with the idea of it being my swan song'.

Crace did not immediately fire off his proposal to Melbourne. Since mid-June his flag had been transferred to the *Rushcutter* depot and he worked from an office in the Orient Buildings in Spring Street in the city. He remained shore-based for the next six months; clearly time hung heavily on his hands during this period, with his diary regularly carrying entries complaining that he had 'nothing to do', that there was 'little doing in the office', or there was 'not much of interest' happening. In this atmosphere, over the next three weeks, he refined and developed his scheme for what he described as 'the elimination of Crace'.

The idea which Crace planned to put to the Naval Board was for the amalgamation of his post as flag-officer of the Australian Squadron with that of Commodore-in-Charge at Sydney (CCS) holding responsibility for the large naval establishment focused on that port. This was, he considered, the best means of providing him with a reasonable and worthwhile job during periods when dispersion of the Australian Squadron meant there was no requirement for a commanding admiral. He realised that such a move did nothing for the CCS post, since it reduced that officer's status by robbing him of his duties and authority only until the squadron concentrated and RACAS was required to go to sea again. And unless such an arrangement was permanent there was no opportunity to effect a saving in personnel. In Crace's view the ideal solution was simply to let him go home, as he was redundant while ever the Naval Board retained operational control. In such circumstances it seemed preferable to him that the Board should assume responsibility for the administration of the squadron as well, let the senior captain take command of the ships, and do without a flag-officer at all.

By early August Crace had polished his scheme and formally proposed it to Royle. It was not until late in the month that he had a chance of personally discussing the idea with CNS, during a visit to Navy Office at which the vexed question of operational control was also raised. At this meeting Royle seemed open to persuasion on both issues, though he made clear that he favoured centralised control and was less than sympathetic to the amalgamation idea. Nonetheless, on 3 September he finally advised Crace that he was turning him down.

Having lost this bid to be allowed a credible job to do, Crace could only hope that his tenure as a flag-officer-without-authority would be prolonged not a moment longer than necessary. The news which the Naval Board received on 6 October, advising that the Admiralty proposed extending Crace's appointment until about April 1942, must therefore have seemed like the last straw for him. London was apparently unaware of the serious depths to which matters had sunk and was presumably swayed more by evidence that Crace had been a great success in the RACAS post. Tributes to his personal style were being paid not just in private but also in public. The *Bulletin* held that he had proved to be 'well liked in the R.A.N. and his methods admirably suit its temperament', and another publication had commented approvingly: 'Efficient in himself, looking for efficiency in others but, above all, just and fair in his treatment of all hands, "R.A.C.A.S." ... has won a high place in the affections and esteem of those who serve under him.'

To the Board's credit, it neither attempted to hold Crace further against his will nor let him go in terms which might seem injurious to his good name. In a very fair reply, it concurred in the proposed extension but stated that Crace wished to revert to the Royal Navy as soon as possible after his loan engagement expired, and suggested that a relief officer should leave for Australia at the earliest opportunity.

With the realisation that there was now no prospect of his replacement arriving by 1 November, Crace found his position *vis-*

à-vis the Board only getting worse. Less than a week after the advice from the Admiralty things were at crisis point. On 9–10 October there had been an exchange of signals between Navy Office and Crace regarding the detailing of squadron vessels as escorts to various transports. Crace took strong exception to receiving instructions that he assign specific cruisers to covering these separate movements, considering that this was effectively telling him how to do his job. In what he admitted to his diary was a 'pretty acrimonious chat', on 11 October he spoke by telephone to Captain Frank Getting, Deputy CNS at Navy Office, objecting to the Board's 'intolerable interference' in his duties and insisting that the Board should send him a signal either directing him to comply with their instructions or else giving him a free hand to deal with the matter as he saw fit.

Realising what would flow from telling Crace to comply with instructions in a matter for which he held operational responsibility, the Board chose not to send the signal he demanded. But nor did it concede his right to exercise his own judgement in a matter of this sort free from the interference of the naval staff. In the circumstances Crace decided that there was only one thing he could do. As it happened Royle was in Sydney, staying at Government House, so Crace made an appointment to see him there the next morning, Sunday 12 October.

At the meeting Crace began by apologising to Royle for dropping a bombshell on him but stated that it was his intention to resign the post of RACAS the next morning. He recounted the history of the battle over operational control, adding that the Board had also been evincing a lack of confidence in his administration by such actions as altering the punishments he awarded in disciplinary cases brought before him. In Crace's account of the hour-long scene which followed (he called it a 'seance'), he records that both became pretty heated, with Royle telling Crace that he could not resign in wartime and that if he did send in his resignation he (Royle) would tear it up:

> The old argument that I might be wanted to take the squadron to sea at any time was advanced and that I could not be spared. I think he understands my feelings and was not speaking honestly when he said it was pure selfishness on my part wanting to leave. Anyhow he ended by saying he appreciated my coming to him before taking the step and assured me he would find a job for me and urged me to possess my soul in patience.

Crace can scarcely have been satisfied with the outcome of this attempt to achieve a resolution of the main issue, especially as it still left him without any meaningful function. He had Royle's promise to find him useful employment, but he already had an inkling of what this might mean. In early August there had been a port-call to Brisbane by the American cruisers *Salt Lake City* and *Northampton*, and it was Crace who was sent off to entertain the visitors as the representative of the Minister for the Navy and the Naval Board. The occasion had been in no way onerous, and ultimately it would prove a useful introduction to a future ally. Crace was perhaps agreeably surprised at how easily good relations had been established with the Americans, particularly their commander, Rear-Admiral S. A. Taffinder, whom he found to be 'most charming and very easy to get on with—full of quiet and subtle humour'. But for an underemployed flag-officer activities like this were no substitute for real command duties.

The idea of finding something for Crace to do may have been partly responsible for the task that came his way a month after his fiery interview with Royle. On 19 November, off the west Australian coast, HMAS *Sydney* had encountered the heavily-armed German auxiliary cruiser *Kormoran* which had been preying on Allied shipping in the Indian Ocean. In the ensuing action, which still holds many mysteries for naval historians, the enemy raider was sunk but with the loss of the Australian cruiser as well. There were 318 survivors rescued from the *Kormoran*, but the *Sydney* had disappeared along with her entire complement of 645 men.

While an intensive air and sea search was mounted for the missing cruiser, no official announcement was made until 30 November. By this time, however, the rumour-mill had been busy and reports circulated Australia-wide that a major RAN unit had been lost. Crace was quickly caught up in this tragic business. He was apparently unaware of initial alarm in naval circles that he was himself a victim of the cruiser's disappearance. In her book Barbara Winter records that there was an anxious exchange of cipher telegrams following a report that RACAS had been lost aboard *Sydney*, until it was confirmed that Crace was in Sydney town, not *Sydney* ship. He became directly involved after his wife went to play bridge with Lady Fairfax several days before the announcement and was asked by her hostess whether it was true that the *Australia* had been sunk. In view of the generous hospitality the Fairfaxes had previously shown to him and Carola, he

37

was greatly embarrassed at feeling obliged to send a naval intelligence officer around to enquire about the source of this information. In what had been an awkward interview Lady Fairfax insisted that she heard the news on a tram.

Amid the atmosphere of shock associated with such a severe blow, naval authorities were anxious to establish precisely what had occurred during the *Sydney–Kormoran* clash; virtually the only means of doing so was through interrogation of the German survivors who had been picked up afterwards and were now being held as prisoners of war in Western Australia. Crace was evidently rather surprised — as well he might be — when he received instructions to proceed to Fremantle and take personal charge of the conduct of the interrogation process.

The reasons given by Captain Getting at Navy Office for his being detailed for this work were his seniority, the fact that *Sydney* had been one of his ships, and a desire on the part of the naval authorities to prevent the army from butting in. Crace heard other reports of friction between Captain Charles Farquhar-Smith (the naval officer in charge in Western Australia) and Getting, and complaints that the interrogation had not been conducted very satisfactorily up to this point. There was also no unanimity at Navy Office about Crace going, as he soon discovered. When he rang Durnford, the Second Naval Member of the Board, to tell him of his departure plans for the west, he was now implored to stay where he was — the Far Eastern situation was judged to be most critical and war expected at any moment. Crace was disinclined to alter his plans even for this contingency, noting in his diary: 'Even so I can't see that I can be of much help with only two ships here.' He could not, in any event, exercise a personal preference in the matter. His presence had been directed by CNS, who was disturbed at the credence being given by the interrogation team already assembled to obvious lies being told by German crew members.

Flying into Perth on 30 November, Crace was driven to the Swanbourne army barracks the next morning. With the assistance of two interpreters, he began personally interviewing the 19 officers being held from the *Kormoran*. He had brought with him a list of subjects on which to direct his questioning, this list having been drawn up for him by the Naval Board and handed to him as he passed through Melbourne *en route*, but as he confided to his diary, 'We could get little of real value out of them.' While it was possible to reconstruct a reasonable description of the action between the raider and the cruiser, it appeared that no-one definitely knew the final fate of the *Sydney* nor why there had been not a single survivor from it. After battering each other with shellfire for half an hour, the two ships had drifted apart, crippled and ablaze. With fires in its engine-room, the *Kormoran* had been abandoned and scuttled by the crew in the early evening, and the German survivors alleged that all they knew of *Sydney* was that it had last been seen as a glare in the darkness which finally disappeared from view around midnight.

After this first day Crace was convinced that he could not be of any real use here, and proposed allowing the questioning to continue under a naval officer other than himself, with the two interpreters. If he could get this system going satisfactorily, he decided he would head back east within a few days. While these arrangements were being put into place, he involved himself with another wretched consequence of the presumed sinking of the *Sydney* — the writing of 650 letters of condolence to the families of the missing crew. Crace initially thought to take this task directly upon himself, getting up at 5.30am on 3 December to make a start. Later that morning, having completed 90 letters at a rate of only 17½ per hour, he gave up. 'My fingers were so sore & my brain buzzing so much that I then went out and enquired about getting facsimile letters done . . . I shall not get them done otherwise.'

Crace was returning from his time in Western Australia during the first week of December 1941 when the advice previously given him about the imminence of the long-expected eruption of war in the Pacific proved to be correct. Reaching Melbourne on Saturday 7 December, he was enjoying a drink with Getting at the Menzies Hotel when his companion took an urgent telephone call requiring his presence at Navy Office; accompanying Getting, Crace heard that a well-escorted Japanese convoy was steering into the Gulf of Siam. Arriving back in Sydney by air later the next day, he was at home when the telephone rang at 7 o'clock on Monday morning and he learnt of the almost simultaneous attacks launched by Japan across South-East Asia and the Pacific. Although the news was sketchy on 8 December, it would soon be known that the Japanese had struck against the American Pacific Fleet base at Pearl Harbour in Hawaii, the United States Pacific territories of Wake Island and Guam, the Philippines, Kota Bharu in Malaya, Singora and Patani in Thailand, and Hong Kong. For Crace, the period of longing for worthwhile employment was at an end.

4 Impertinent Allies

W ITH Japan's entry into the war and the start of full-scale hostilities in Australia's strategic environs, the immediate problem for naval authorities was to get RAN units serving overseas back for home defence as quickly as possible. *Australia* was on its way to Fremantle from the Cape, but *Kanimbla* and *Manoora* were at Singapore and *Hobart* and *Yarra* were in the Mediterranean. *Canberra* and *Perth*, berthed at Sydney, put to sea for gunnery trials in the next few days, before being ordered on 12 December to proceed to Brisbane where they arrived three days later.

Crace joined the two cruisers by air the same day, hoisting his flag in *Canberra*. He then sailed for New Caledonia, in anticipation of this Free French territory becoming the target of another Japanese landing. As he advised in signals sent to Navy Office in Melbourne, and to naval authorities in Wellington and other ships in the area, a direction-finding bearing obtained during the evening of 13 December indicated an enemy transport in a position which placed it in a direct line between Truk and the Solomon Islands. Appreciating that this raised the 'possibility of enemy attempt to land in New Caledonia or vicinity, probably 18 December', he now made it his object 'to defeat any attempt by enemy to consolidate himself in New Caledonia area'.

By placing his force in the vicinity of New Caledonia, Crace was also providing cover for several important friendly ship movements, including the troopship *Ormiston* travelling from Sydney to Noumea, the capital of New Caledonia, and the *Wahine* taking troops from Auckland to Fiji. Also a prime consideration was the safe passage of an American convoy of seven merchant ships escorted by the heavy cruiser USS *Pensacola*. This had sailed from Hawaii a week before the Japanese attack, bound for Manila with supplies and reinforcements for US forces stationed in the Philippines. On board were 2600 members of the US Army Air Corps, including 48 pilots, and 90 aircraft, as well as 2000 troops of two field artillery regiments, with their guns. Diverted to Fiji by Japan's entry into the war, the convoy was now making for Brisbane with instructions that, if it was impossible to proceed to the original destination, the troops and equipment should be used in 'aiding the Allies of the U.S.A.'.

The Australian cruisers joined up with the American ships on 19 December, finding the latter already in company with the New Zealand cruiser *Achilles*, also detailed to assist. In the words of a New Zealand account:

> . . . we carried on towards Brisbane in tropical weather which had us stripped of unessentials while looking for draughty spots about our upperdecks. *Pensacola*'s four aircraft ranged about the horizon with those from our cruisers on constant patrol, being joined on Sunday by 13 Hudsons from Queensland fields right until we entered Moreton Bay to refuel.

The convoy being brought safely to its new destination on 22 December, the Australian cruisers made for Sydney later that same day. Arriving on Christmas Eve, they found HMAS *Australia* had reached port three days before. Crace now made *Australia* his flagship, it being the more modern of the heavy cruisers. He brought with him as his flag captain and chief staff officer Captain Harold Farncomb, who now changed places with Captain George Moore, transferred to command *Canberra*. A member of the original entry into Australia's naval college when it opened in 1913, Farncomb held the distinction of having become in June 1937 the first graduate of the college to attain captain's rank.

On 28 December Crace sailed with his three Australian cruisers and *Achilles* to provide an escort to three transports carrying reinforcements and equipment to New Guinea. After seeing these troops and stores ashore at Port Moresby on 3 January 1942, Crace the next day took his squadron (less *Canberra*, left to accompany one of the discharged transports back to Sydney) to the Free French territory of New Caledonia. Their departure coincided with the Japanese bombing of Rabaul, 440 nautical miles to the north-east of Moresby. Arriving at Noumea on 7 January, the warships remained there for two days to provide temporary anti-aircraft protection for the town, then departed to escort another convoy of troopships

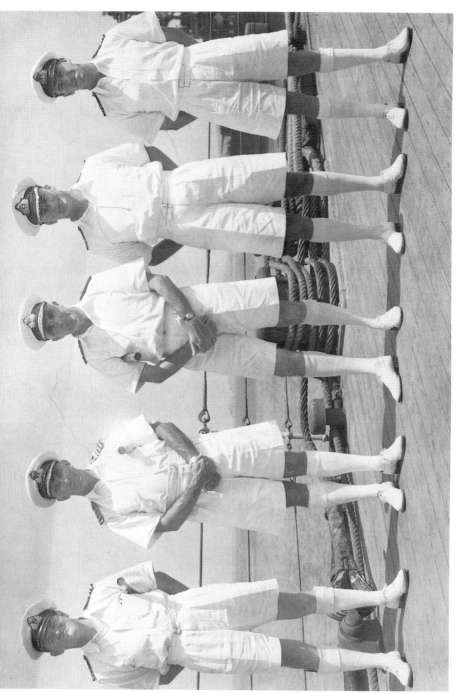

Crace (centre) with his staff, taken during the first months of 1942: (from left) Lieutenant-Commander John Bath (Flag Lieutenant-Commander and squadron communications officer), Captain Harold Farncomb (Flag Captain and chief staff officer), Paymaster Commander Pat Perry (Admiral's Secretary), and Lieutenant-Commander George Oldham (Staff Officer (Operations & Intelligence)). (*Rev. J. A. Crace*)

bound for Suva, Fiji. With the completion of this task, the squadron returned to Sydney to await developments.

At this point Australian authorities were alarmed that the Australian coastline was excluded from the naval zone in the Pacific for which the US Navy proposed to undertake defence responsibility. Under an agreement reached between the Australian and American governments on 27 January, a new entity was to be set up covering the north-eastern portion of the Australian Station and which would be separate from the ABDA (American-British-Dutch-Australian) naval area which had been formed taking in the north-western approaches. The new area would be known as 'Anzac Area' and patrolled by an Allied naval force called 'Anzac Force'.

Crace was aware of these proposed arrangements, having been in discussion with Royle at Navy Office on 21 January when CNS read out a cable from Washington regarding the Anzac Force. Although it was intended that it would comprise some 23 ships from Britain, the United States and New Zealand, as well as Australia, the RAN was to contribute 16 of these (two heavy cruisers, one light cruiser, three armed merchant cruisers, two destroyers, two anti-submarine patrol vessels and six locally-built corvettes). The Americans were offering to provide just one 8-inch or 6-inch cruiser, yet proposed that a US flag officer should command the whole force. Crace thought this a colossal impertinence on their part, but philosophically observed that 'we've got to take what we can get nowadays'.

On 27 January the squadron—now including HMAS *Adelaide*—sailed out of harbour, heading north-east to link up with another west-bound convoy. They were returning to Sydney when Crace learnt that *Perth* was being detached to the ABDA area in a week's time. Fuming, he recorded his response to this news in his diary:

> This is maddening and must be I think an overruling of N.B. [Naval Board] opinion by Government. Perth cannot make all the difference to ABDA whereas her loss here makes this force inadequate for its job ... We must concentrate & if there is to be a force in Anzac Area it should be big enough for its job of Trade protection & capable of dealing with a Japanese landing force in the Islands. If this cannot be provided then the Cruiser Force in Anzac waters should go complete to ABDA. We shall be eaten up piece meal if the present policy of having a few ships everywhere is continued. Sent at long cypher to N.B. in the above sense.

Arriving in Sydney on 31 January, Crace now heard about signals which had been exchanged regarding the establishment of Anzac

Area. It was believed that the US proposed 'taking over everything here including coastal convoys' and that the new area commander was to be shore-based. This was doubtless a relief to Crace, but raised a question over the role that the CNS in Melbourne would fulfil in this case. Crace also learnt that he might well lose his flag-captain, Farncomb, as chief of staff to the new US admiral when he arrived.

Later the same day, *Australia* put to sea again to cover more shipping movements in the Tasman Sea. During the night a message was received with the news that Rear-Admiral Herbert Leary USN had been appointed to command Anzac Force and promoted to the rank of vice-admiral. Crace was now ordered to proceed at speed to Wellington, arriving two days later.

On 7 February, Leary flew into Wellington with a nucleus staff and formally took over command of Anzac Area under the short title of COMANZAC. In discussions with the New Zealand Naval Board and Crace about the proposed operational and administrative organisation of the area, he stated his intention to establish his headquarters at Navy Office, Melbourne. He also directed Crace to assume command of the seagoing squadron of Anzac Force, which Crace did on 12 February at Suva, the port agreed upon as the squadron's advanced operational base. The functions laid down for the Anzac Squadron were:

> To seek out and destroy inferior enemy forces, remaining on the defensive and acting as a stop gap force until such time as the area could be reinforced. To retire at all times in the face of superior enemy forces, particularly those including aircraft carriers, and generally in a north-easterly direction with the object of gaining air support from Fiji and general support from Task Force 11. And to ensure the safe arrival of US convoys and generally give cover support for trans-Pacific movements.

As Crace now discovered, the ships actually available for the formation of his squadron were just the heavy cruisers *Australia* (flagship) and USS *Chicago*, the light cruisers *Achilles* and *Leander* from New Zealand, and two American destroyers (*Perkins* and *Lamson*). *Canberra* had entered an extensive refit, and other RAN units earmarked for the new entity were diverted, at least temporarily, to duties elsewhere. At Suva, Crace linked up with the US and New Zealand components of his squadron, all having arrived there from Brisbane, Pearl Harbour, Auckland and Wellington within a space of seven hours.

Exchange of signal personnel between HMAS *Australia* and USS *Chicago* facilitated communications between the main units of Crace's Anzac Squadron. This photograph shows a RAN rating (right) working with US sailors on the signal bridge of the American heavy cruiser.
(*Mr F. Timmerman*)

The formation of an Allied squadron brought new requirements and experiences. The *Chicago* was in most respects comparable to Crace's flagship, displacing 9200 tons and carrying nine 8-inch guns as its main armament (as against *Australia*'s 10 000 tons and eight 8-inch guns); but in September 1940 it had become the first US cruiser to be fitted with the new CXAM radar, carrying in its mainmast a huge unwieldy framework which provided a first glimpse of radar equipment for RAN personnel who had not been away from the Australian Station. Before undertaking operations with American units and formations, the Australians had to learn and adopt the signals and operating procedures of the US Navy. The transition from the British 'Fleet Signal Book' to the American 'General Signal Book' was reportedly accomplished in just 48 hours, aided by several signallers transferred to the flagship from the *Chicago*. Among these was Petty Officer Frank Westley, who recalls:

I stood bridge watches, helping her officers and crew with our ship and aircraft identification, also helping to interpret the difference between our two countries' signals that were necessary with flags and semaphore during the day watch, and with light signals after dark.

Seven RAN signal ratings were also drafted to the US cruiser on 13 February to help coordinate communications, along with a lieutenant-commander sent to act as liaison officer. The transfer of skills was, however, unlikely to have been entirely a one-way affair, and as Frances Maguire remarked: 'The Australian contribution to the development of tactics and the growth of the Force should not be forgotten.'

Crace began to get to know the American commanders with whom he would be working, particularly the heavy cruiser's Captain Howard Bode (pronounced 'Boadee'). Two years Crace's junior, he had enjoyed a varied career since graduating from the US naval academy in 1907. With extensive service in submarines, he was—like Crace—a torpedo specialist, had spent long years serving on the China Station, and as well had been assistant military attaché in US embassies in Berlin, Stockholm, Copenhagen, The Hague, Rome, Paris and London. In command of the battleship *Oklahoma* when that vessel became a casualty of the Japanese attack on Pearl Harbour, he had assumed command of the *Chicago* a month later and was still relatively new to his ship. Bode was, moreover, a difficult personality—it even being asserted that he was the inspiration for the psychotic captain in Thomas Heggen's novel *Mister Roberts*, later adapted into a play and a motion picture. This aspect of Bode's character is confirmed by Petty Officer Westley, who was his 'writer' or clerk:

> Captain Bode was a very unhappy officer . . . Senior officers in the U.S. Navy often referred to him as Captain Bligh of the mutiny on the Bounty, and Captain Bode seemed to like this . . . [He] was disliked by most, but was a strong disciplinarian and most officers and men showed respect.

While the potential apparently existed for Australian-American relations to come under some strain from this association, in fact a remarkably good relationship was quickly established. As Westley notes, Bode displayed 'high respect for Admiral Crace. More than he had for most officers . . . He seemed to have little respect for any person or their feelings, but there appeared to be some mystic relationship when he referred to the Admiral.' That Crace was able to work harmoniously with such a stern critic was certainly something of a tribute to his professional capabilities, and also his skills in handling interpersonal relations.

Interestingly, however, the basis for the mutual trust and regard between the two men was apparently laid by Bode, who took the initiative in demonstrating his willingness to be entirely candid with his Australian superior. While showing Crace over the *Chicago* (or 'Cagow' as she was dubbed) on 13 February, Bode had shown him a signal which the ship's operators had intercepted passing from Admiral Ernest King, Commander-in-Chief of the US Fleet, in Washington, to Leary. This revealed that King considered it desirable for Leary to embark in his flagship at once, and take both his own Anzac Force and another US task force being despatched to him to carry out a more offensive policy. In his diary Crace noted that this looked bad for him, as with Leary afloat he would become redundant and could expect to be displaced. There was no immediate follow-up to this signal, which Crace and Bode agreed probably indicated that Leary had countered by cabling Washington with the view that he could best control the Anzac Area from ashore. Confirmation that Leary was resisting the attempt to make him embark was received a day or so later, and Crace was able to breathe more easily.

Anzac Squadron sailed on 14 February, and two days later linked up with US Task Force 11 commanded by Vice-Admiral Wilson Brown. The principal battle unit of this force was the majestic aircraft carrier *Lexington* — the 'Lady Lex' as it was affectionately known to those who sailed in it. Although already 15 years old, this ship was a formidable and impressive emblem of sea-power, carrying some 90 aircraft and a crew of 3300 officers and men. Despite its giant size — it was nearly 900 feet long and displaced 33 000 tons — its 16 boilers, the uptakes of which were combined into a single massive smokestack 79 feet high, drove her along at 33 knots.

With her escort of four cruisers (*Indianapolis, Minneapolis, Pensacola* and *San Francisco*) and ten modern destroyers, the *Lexington* had been temporarily added to Anzac Force. Admiral Leary, glad to have this major augmentation of strength, had begun planning a heavy air strike against Rabaul, which the Japanese had occupied late the previous month. It was to discuss arrangements for this operation that Crace now prepared to board the carrier. With

16 February 1942, and Anzac Squadron links up with US Task Force 11
led by the aircraft carrier *Lexington* in preparation for an attack on
Japanese-held Rabaul; Crace transferred to the carrier by barge for a
conference with the US commander, Vice-Admiral Wilson Brown. (*Cdre
D. H. D. Smyth*)

Lexington's aircraft constantly patrolling overhead, and the seven-
teen warships of the two forces cruising in company in two long
columns led by the *Australia*, Crace went across to the carrier in his
barge for a conference lasting into the mid-afternoon. Returning to
his flagship, Crace led his squadron back towards Suva while Task
Force 11 continued towards the north-west.

During the meeting aboard the *Lexington* Crace was given
Brown's operation orders setting out the plan of attack, and he was
less than happy with what he learnt. In cooperating with Task
Force 11 his ships were assigned only a secondary role. As he
irritably wrote in his diary, for the forthcoming attack Brown had
given him 'the dreary task of escorting and protecting his oiler and
acting in support of him'. The Anzac Squadron was to patrol a line
between Suva and Noumea, and escort the oiler *Platte* to a rendezvous where the carrier force could refuel after the air strike on
Rabaul.

Crace had not been disposed to take what he regarded as 'a poor affair' lying down, and had objected to Brown that he was out there to 'shoot Japs' and not to 'chaperone a blooming oiler'. He obtained no satisfaction with this protest, but, having made his point, he dutifully put a positive face on matters when he gave his briefing about the squadron's forthcoming role. Addressing his officers in the flagship at 9am on 19 February, he stressed the importance of getting the tanker to the designated position because without re-fuelling facilities the operation would fail. Anzac Squadron's task was therefore important, and he expected everyone to do their 'damnedest' to ensure success. Ending by expressing confidence in the squadron, he spoke of his pride and pleasure in flying his flag in a ship which was 'the namesake of [the] ship I served in as T.L. [Torpedo Lieutenant] 27 years ago in these waters.'

With news of the British surrender at Singapore fresh upon them, the ships of Anzac Squadron embarked on their assigned task of escorting the *Platte*, deep-laden with 17 000 tons of fuel. As the chronicler of HMNZS *Achilles* records:

> *Platte* sat low in the Pacific, mole-ploughing an 18-knot creamy furrow through which *Lamson* and *Perkins* capered in the usual manner of destroyers at sea. *Australia* forged ahead of *Chicago* to starboard of our oiler, while to port we yawed gracefully in *Leander*'s wake, being brought back into line by our helmsman as he corrected against a lazily swinging compass pointer.

The only excitement which the mission generated came about not from enemy activity but from mishaps to the squadron's aircraft, which were on constant anti-submarine patrol. At noon on 19 February *Australia*'s amphibian was gliding in to make a 'slick landing' (a practised procedure in which the big cruiser turned through the wind to create a patch of calm water onto which the aircraft was put down). On this occasion, however, the pilot mis-judged his distance and collided with the ship's stern, just above the water line. The plane broke up and, falling astern of the slowly-steaming flagship, burst into flames and quickly sank. Boats were immediately lowered by the *Australia*, but it was a motorboat from the *Chicago* which reached the spot first and picked up the two survivors, the pilot's body going down with the wreckage.

By the next morning the weather had worsened, and the squad-ron ploughed on in a heavy swell during which a man was lost overboard from the *Lamson*. These conditions added to the hazards posed for the aircraft which were maintaining patrols. While land-ing that afternoon, *Leander*'s aircraft was damaged and temporarily put out of action; *Achilles*'s aircraft, which had been taken on board the flagship after the previous day's mishap to take advantage of the superior handling conditions available on the bigger ship, also sustained slight damage on landing; and one of *Chicago*'s aircraft, sent on a subsequent patrol, overturned while attempting to land alongside its parent ship and sank, fortunately without loss of its crew. With rain now setting in during the night, the escorting cruisers formed a diamond around the tanker.

Although Anzac Squadron did its assignment, and in the words of the US official history 'did it well', the strike was unsuccessful. On the morning of 20 February, Japanese reconnaissance aircraft from Rabaul spotted the approaching carrier force while it was still 18 hours sailing time away from the point where Brown planned to send off the aircraft making the attack. That afternoon, air attacks were launched against the carrier force by two waves of nine twin-engine bombers, which—incredibly—sortied without fighter cover. According to the American pilots, this cost the Japanese 16 of the attacking aircraft shot down and another damaged, all for the loss of just two US planes and one pilot. Such claims were often wildly optimistic, but in this case the reports of heavy enemy loss could be broadly verified, as the air combat took place directly above the task force. To the men on the ships it seemed they held first-class seats to a new form of spectator sport, and there was wild barracking for the home team. Admiral Brown later said: 'I even had to remind some members of my staff that this was not a football game.' At one point a downed enemy bomber attempted to crash into the carrier as it fell, but when the action was over no damage had been inflicted on the American force. Nonetheless, the element of surprise had clearly been forfeited and Brown conse-quently called off the attack.

By late afternoon on 22 February Anzac Squadron linked up with Task Force 11 and took up station on Brown's starboard bow. In the wake of the aborted Rabaul raid, it was agreed by the two com-manders that Brown's force would commence patrolling in and around the Coral Sea, while Crace took his squadron firstly to Suva and then to Noumea, now to be regarded as the Anzac Force's advanced operational base. After refuelling, the squadron would rejoin Task Force 11 west of the New Hebrides on 3 March. Before making this separation, Brown invited Crace's views on the shape and nature of their future cooperation upon rejoining the two forces. He did so in the light of a suggestion from Leary that they should return to the offensive as soon as both forces had completed fuelling.

In his response, sent in a letter delivered to *Lexington* on 23 February, Crace expressed his belief that the Coral Sea was where they should both operate and that it was essential that the two forces work as a combined force or at least in the closest cooperation. He disagreed strongly, however, with Brown's idea of the Anzac Squadron acting as a 'full-back' on a line between Suva and Noumea, arguing that his ships would be out of reach and short of fuel when required to support Task Force 11.

Later the same day, Brown sent back a reply in which he expressed disagreement with COMANZAC's suggested 'return to the attack' immediately refuelling was done. He did, however, agree with Crace's appreciation that Port Moresby, New Caledonia, Fiji and the Ellice Islands (in that order) were probably the next eastern objectives of the Japanese, and that the strongest position for the Allied squadrons was in the Coral Sea, from where they should be able to detect and oppose any enemy move in force. He also accepted that, on its return, Anzac Force should work with his task force in one of three roles (either advanced screen, striking force, or outer screen), stating that:

> ... we should concentrate our naval strength so far as fuel needs will permit. It is unfortunate that we must be so hampered by that primary requirement. It was only in order that you might have sufficient fuel at the appropriate time that I suggested the Suva-Noumea area as your general theatre of operations rather than cruising habitually as support with this Task Force.

Despite this evident degree of accord, in fact there remained a niggling tension between the two commanders. After reaching Suva on 26 February, where the news was received of heavy Japanese air raids on Darwin, *Australia* and *Chicago* went to Noumea for refuelling. Leaving there on 1 March accompanied by *Lamson*, the cruisers linked up the next day with the US tanker *Kaskaskia* escorted by *Perkins* and proceeded to the position arranged for the rendezvous with Task Force 11 on 3 March. Two days later, the US destroyers of Anzac Force were detached on Brown's orders, causing Crace to remark in his diary: 'I don't like our Destroyers being taken away as they have just got used to us. It looks as if the Anzac Force was to be treated as odd man out rather. I'll just have to wait & see & do as I'm told this time I think.' The next day, however, he found an opportunity to indicate his views on the matter, recording that:

> I had hinted gently that I felt the removal of my destroyers & the reply was that they were selected as being short of fuel! (a defect very easily remedied & an excuse of the very feeblest). I have a horrid feeling that instead of using Anzac Force as an attacking force we are to be kept with the Carrier. That will be too awful.

At this time intelligence reports suggested that the Japanese fleet had withdrawn from Rabaul, a move which Brown believed might indicate an impending attack on either Port Moresby or the Solomon Islands. It appears that Crace, whose image with the Americans is encapsulated by his description in the US official history as 'that energetic warrior', had been urging Brown to undertake offensive action in terms which the latter regarded as somewhat impertinent. Brown wrote to Crace on 3 March, telling him that another major US naval force had been ordered to join them three days later at a point 300 miles north of Noumea. This was Task Force 17 commanded by Rear-Admiral Frank Fletcher. The principal combat unit of this force was the aircraft carrier *Yorktown*, escorted by two heavy cruisers (*Astoria* and *Louisville*) and seven destroyers. A more modern ship than the 'Lady Lex', having been launched only in 1936, *Yorktown* was considerably smaller (displacing 20 000 tons as against *Lexington*'s 33 000) yet was capable of carrying 100 aircraft. Brown went on to observe that, although instructions had been given for the naval forces in the Anzac Area to 'carry out an offensive role whenever opportunity presents itself rather than a passive protection of army units', it appeared to him that:

> . . . an opportunity for offensive action by us will present itself only when and if the enemy initiate offensive action in our area. I repeat that I consider his air position around Rabaul, combined with the physical geographic difficulties of successful surprise approach, too formidable to warrant risking two of our three carriers in the Pacific.

Notwithstanding Brown's reply, when the rendezvous with the *Yorktown* force was made as scheduled, the whole of this combined armada now prepared to embark on precisely the sort of operation which Brown appeared to have just previously told Crace was unthinkable. On 6 March a convoy carrying an American force of

16 000 men which was to garrison New Caledonia left Melbourne; to cover the final leg of its movement from Brisbane to Noumea, Brown was ordered to prepare a second attack on Rabaul.

To comply with this instruction he planned to mount simultaneous attacks against Rabaul and Gasmata, on the southern coast of New Britain. The two towns were to be visited by strong forces of bombers before dawn on 9 March, followed by bombardments by cruisers at daybreak. The available cruisers would be divided into three groups: one staying to protect the carriers; a second (Task Group 11.8) to bombard Rabaul; the third (Task Group 11.9) to shell Gasmata.

Because of his forebodings about his force being held back in a purely supporting role with the carriers, and knowing that a big operation was in the offing, Crace decided that he should make his views known directly to Brown before it was too late. He accordingly asked to see the task force commander and secured an appointment for 8am on 7 March. In his account of the interview, Crace records that he began by asking Brown how his squadron was to be employed in the forthcoming operation. On being told that the cruisers *Australia* and *Chicago*, with two destroyers, were to comprise the task group attacking Gasmata he was most satisfied, saying that he had feared a policy of keeping his ships with the carriers might have had repercussions for morale in his flagship, also on public opinion in Australia, and possibly politically:

> I said 'After all it is our . . .' he interjected 'war' . . . and I concluded 'Territory and we have been fighting this war for 2½ years'! He said he fully realised these facts and had taken them into account in formulating his plans.

Though pleased to have been allocated at last an active part to play in an operation, Crace's satisfaction did not last for long. While on the way to deliver the planned attacks, it was learnt that the Japanese had made landings at Lae and Salamaua on the north coast of the New Guinea mainland. Brown immediately altered his plan, deciding now to enter the Gulf of Papua with his carriers and send aircraft over the Owen Stanleys, the lofty mountain range forming the spine of Papua and New Guinea, to attack the new landing sites in the hope of catching the enemy unprepared. Under these changed arrangements, the attack groups 11.8 and 11.9 were combined as a new Task Group 11.7 under Crace's command and given the role of attacking surface forces 'when directed'. As Crace

53

instantly realised, this actually meant that 'we shall not do anything at all'.

Crace was strongly of the opinion that Brown's reversal of plan was a mistake, observing in his diary: 'As Rabaul is the nest he should have maintained it as his chief objective and let the surface forces go for Salamaua and Lae.' He wondered if the failure of the last attempt on Rabaul had shaken Brown's nerve so that 'he does not like the idea this time'. Crace's unhappiness at the turn of events was only compounded when he received the orders for the new operation on 9 March, because under these it emerged he had been given merely a role of passive support for a second time. Though 'again loudly protesting at missing a chance to "shoot Japs"', as the US official history put it, there was nothing he could do about it.

5 *Distractions*

AUGMENTED by the US cruisers *Astoria* and *Louisville*, and the destroyers *Anderson, Hammann, Hughes* and *Sims*, the group led by Crace was sent eastward shortly before midday on 9 March to patrol off the Louisiade Archipelago. Its task was to act as a screen against any sudden Japanese move which might threaten the troop convoy making for New Caledonia or the carrier force while it was in the Gulf, and again to escort the oilers *Neosho* and *Kaskaskia* to a fuelling rendezvous.

The next morning 104 aircraft were launched by the two carriers from a point about 45 miles off the Papuan coast. Using a cloud-free pass through the 15 000-foot peaks of the Owen Stanleys, the attack formations reached the northern coast and turned north-west towards the two target towns along the Huon Gulf. Complete surprise was achieved against the unsuspecting enemy. First reaching Salamaua, an isthmus settlement about 25 miles south of Lae, the aircraft found an abundance of shipping in the harbour and attacked in strafing, bombing and torpedo runs. Although the Japanese had, immediately after capturing Lae, set about preparing the airfield there to receive fighter aircraft from Rabaul, these had not yet arrived. Accordingly the only air protection available to the Japanese came from the aircraft on a seaplane tender. Even so, it was observed that torpedoes from the *Lexington*'s bombers did not run very well, with the result that the success of the American fliers was minor. Japanese sources available after the war showed that only two transports (*Kongo Maru* and *Yokohama Maru*), a converted minelayer (*Tenyo Maru*) and a converted minesweeper (*Tama Maru No. 2*) were sunk, although another seven ships—including the cruiser *Yubari*—suffered some damage. This result was achieved at the cost of only one American aircraft and its two-man crew, despite the Japanese belief that they had shot down eleven planes.

Brown resisted proposals for a second strike during the afternoon, considering it too risky for the carriers to remain longer in their advanced position. This decision was actually most wise, as three large Japanese planes sent from Rabaul about noon to patrol off the north-eastern tip of Australia sighted 'one aircraft carrier of the *Saratoga*-type [i.e. *Lexington*], and five destroyers', about 90 nautical miles from Port Moresby. Adverse weather caused the Japanese aircraft to cease tracking this task force and return to Rabaul, but had Brown remained longer in the area he clearly risked becoming the target of a counter-strike.

Reports from returning pilots indicated a major blow had been struck against the enemy during the morning raids, and Brown was glad to be able to convey some good news to Hawaii and Washington.This prompted US President Roosevelt to send a special message to Britain's Prime Minister Churchill describing it as 'by all means the best day's work we have had'. In terms of overall impact, however, what had been achieved was realised by Brown and others to be nothing more than a pin-prick against the Japanese advance.

Throughout the operation, Crace had been cruising about 200 miles south-east of Rossel Island. His group provided support for the carriers by mounting air patrols to the east, searching for any sign of enemy movement. This aerial surveillance was undertaken by the seven aircraft borne in the cruisers and carried out under the control of the *Astoria*. Although there was no attempt by the Japanese to disrupt either the Noumea convoy or the carrier operations, Crace nonetheless found his hands unexpectedly full during this time.

At dawn on 10 March the group had launched all aircraft on patrol. Sometime afterwards, one of the *Astoria*'s planes radioed that it had made a forced landing, and the parent cruiser parted company to undertake a search which proved unsuccessful. The new Walrus from the *Australia* was also sent aloft during the day to make a three-hour anti-submarine patrol; on returning at 11.45 am the pilot attempted a slick landing in which the aircraft landed heavily and suffered damage which rendered it unserviceable. Worse was to follow the next day, when four aircraft were launched on patrol. By late afternoon all were overdue, and though the group made smoke and burned searchlights until dark, none of the four returned.

On the evening of 12 March, while Crace was still preoccupied

The scene on HMAS *Australia*'s bridge as the flagship enters Noumea Harbour; (clockwise from left) Lieutenant-Commander John Rayment, Lieutenant-Commander George Oldham, Crace, Captain Harold Farncomb, Lieutenant-Commander John Bath, and Lieutenant Allen Dollard. (*Cdre D. H. D. Smyth*)

with the effort to recover the missing aircraft or at least rescue any surviving crew members, more disturbing news reached him. 'To add to my troubles', he wrote in his diary, Farncomb came to tell him that a stoker on board the flagship had been discovered very badly stabbed and slashed. The next day, Friday 13 March, the task group abandoned its vigil off the Louisiades and altered course for the rendezvous position. At 9.55 pm the injured man, Stoker John Riley, died of peritonitis resulting from his wounds. Crace now had a murder inquiry on his hands.

After the rendezvous with the carriers was made at dawn on 14 March, the two carrier task forces and Crace's ships separated. Brown's *Lexington* force steamed back to its base at Pearl Harbour, while the *Yorktown* group remained in the area with Noumea as its operational base. The squadron, reverting to its designation as Anzac Force and its original strength, sailed for Noumea where the New Zealand cruisers *Achilles* and *Leander* were waiting to join Crace's flag.

The squadron remained in port at Noumea for the next ten days, a period in which the morale of the ships and of Crace personally was severely tested. Even as the squadron was steaming to Noumea the grim news had been received that HMAS *Perth* and HMAS *Yarra* were long overdue and presumed lost to enemy action in waters around Java. Added to the universal depression felt at such terrible losses were the problems arising from the stabbing case aboard the *Australia*. Stoker Riley had been buried at sea at 5pm on 14 March, after a post mortem conducted by a doctor transferred from the *Chicago* and a court of inquiry to obtain medical evidence required for the trial which was certain to follow.

Investigation of the circumstances of the stabbing revealed the full horror of these events. At about 7.40pm Riley had been talking with Acting Leading Stoker Albert Gordon and Stoker Edward Elias in the evening cool of the darkened upper deck. A few minutes later his screams were heard coming from the port side of the Forecastle Deck below B deck; crew members rushing towards the sounds had found Riley covered in blood and writhing in agony, still in the presence of Gordon and Elias. The two stokers maintained that they were merely the first on the scene, having heard Riley's cries when he was set upon moments after leaving their company to go on watch. No other person had been seen leaving the scene by those coming to Riley's assistance, however, and witnesses in positions to view this area of the deck had seen two figures scuffling in the dark with a third man. Gordon and Elias were accordingly placed under close arrest.

Riley's injuries were horrific. He had sustained 14 stab wounds to the chest, abdomen, back and forearms, causing injury to his lungs, liver and intestines. He was taken to the Sick Bay in a critical condition from blood loss and shock, but before he died he stated that Gordon and Elias had attacked him after he threatened to expose them for what Crace referred to in his diary as 'unnatural vice'. As Crace also recorded, the official investigator, Commander John Armstrong, had 'brought to light a large nest of immorality' on the flagship, with three sailors other than the two accused being implicated in homosexual activities. This evidence, collected (as Armstrong admitted) 'under a certain amount of third degree conditions', was, however, only hearsay and inadmissable for legal purposes.

Crace found it difficult to know quite how to handle this matter. In a message to the Naval Board on 15 March he observed that although it seemed to him preferable for the case to be transferred to a civil court, this course appeared impracticable because it could effectively immobilise *Australia*, in view of the 30 personnel who might be needed as witnesses. 'The only alternative', he stated, 'appears to be trial by court martial. In this event I consider it is essential [the] accused should have benefit of [a] good professional adviser to conduct their defence.' He went on to ask that an officer with the required qualifications, if available, be appointed temporarily to the flagship, or some other suitable arrangements made. Above all, bearing in mind the operational movements in prospect for the *Australia*, he stressed that the 'accused should be brought to trial with least delay'.

When the problem was considered at Navy Office, Lieutenant-Commander James Robinson, secretary to the Second Naval Member of the Board, immediately set about establishing on 16 March whether qualified defence counsel was available. He identified two barristers on the staff of the Director of Naval Intelligence, but felt that, in view of the seriousness of the charge, the two accused men 'should have the benefit of the best advice we can make available for them from within the Service'. He therefore suggested enquiries be made to see 'whether there are any other officers serving who have had recent experience in Civil Courts'. In response to this proposal Captain James Foley, secretary to the First Naval Member (the CNS), came up with the name of Paymaster Lieutenant Trevor Rapke, a Naval Reserve officer then at Darwin. Foley described him as a 'criminal lawyer of good standing', having 'conducted the defence in an important case not long ago', and added the final recommendation that 'I would be quite satisfied to have Rapke as my legal adviser if I found myself in trouble'. Rapke was consequently ordered to take passage by air to Townsville at the first opportunity, while Crace was asked to nominate where he should join the *Australia*. Despite Crace's keen insistence that Rapke should proceed to Noumea by the quickest possible means, in the event it was found that there was no early direct flights to Townsville available to him; he was obliged to fly first from Darwin to Adelaide, then travel by rail to Sydney where he caught a Noumea-bound steamer!

At this disturbing juncture letters arrived from Crace's wife which were also unsettling. Carola was tired from the long hours she had been putting into voluntary hospital work and very depressed; she wanted to return home to England. Crace weighed the pros and cons carefully. He judged that notwithstanding the Japanese threat Australia offered greater safety than did England, where the future position was likely to become very unpleasant as the Germans prepared a final effort against the British homeland, and undoubtedly living conditions were better in Australia. Against this it seemed that, if she were to go, it was preferable to leave now while sea travel was relatively safe.

It appeared difficult to Crace to arrive at a decision on this question, but a solution to the dilemma seems to have presented itself a little over a week later when Carola wrote again with news of his replacement. In a conversation with the Governor-General she had been told that 'the bearded VC' might be relieving him as RACAS in June. This was a reference to Rear-Admiral Victor Crutchley, who had won a Victoria Cross in the First World War, wore a full red beard to hide a facial wound scar, and had recently gained prominence as captain of HMS *Warspite* during the Battle at Narvik in Norway. The likelihood that Crace's departure would not be prolonged indefinitely let the question of Carola returning to England on her own rest for the time being.

In the meantime Anzac Squadron put to sea again on 25 March, making for a point north of Fiji to meet up with a convoy bound for the New Hebrides. The convoy was met two days later and escorted to Vila on Efate Island, the squadron taking up patrols in the vicinity while troops were landed and stores unloaded. By 7 April the squadron was heading into the Coral Sea to operate again with Admiral Fletcher's Task Force 17 (*Yorktown*). On 10 April Crace wrote to Fletcher, saying that unless an operation was contemplated for the very near future he proposed to return to Noumea for the court martial on the stabbing case, scheduled to begin in a few days time. The court martial was, he pointed out, very important, and an opportunity to get it out of the way might not recur once the current lull in operations passed, while having it still pending was not good for morale.

Steaming towards New Caledonia the next day, the flagship developed abnormal vibration and a problem was discovered in the starboard outer propeller shaft. At Noumea an inspection revealed that bracket bearings of the affected shaft were badly worn. While this check was being made, the court martial of the two stokers charged with Riley's murder was finally got underway on board the flagship. The opening stage of this proceeding was not without its own drama, with the accused objecting to two of the *Australia's* officers when it came to deciding the membership of the court, on the grounds of possible bias. As finally constituted, the five-man tribunal had on it just two officers from the flagship: Lieutenant-Commander John Bath and Lieutenant-Commander John Rayment, both members of the RAN. The remainder were all RN officers from the New Zealand cruiser *Leander*, including that ship's commanding officer, Captain Robert Bevan (who was appointed president of the court), Commander Stephen Roskill and Lieutenant-Commander Francis Mansell. Captain Farncomb was prosecuting officer.

Following the trial with considerable interest, Crace noted in his diary on 16 April that Rapke, referred to in naval parlance as 'the accused's friend', submitted a plea that there was no case for the stokers to answer and 'apparently made a very good speech to this effect'. This plea was, however, disallowed by the court, and the hearing of evidence continued. Finally, at 11.10am on 18 April, members of the tribunal retired to consider their verdict. At about 3.30pm they returned with a finding that the charges were proved, and Gordon and Elias were sentenced to be hanged 'on board such one of his Majesty's Australian Ships and at such time as the Board of Administration for the Naval Forces shall direct'. When this result was brought to Crace by Captain Bevan, he noted that the president of the court was pretty shaken 'and I don't wonder. Apparently the two accused were unmoved.' He duly signalled the outcome to the Naval Board, and received a reply that on receipt of the minutes of the court proceedings the case 'will be referred to Governor-General in council in accordance with Defence Act Section 98 for confirmation of sentence imposed'. To his diary he confided his private belief that it was 'almost certain that the men will not be executed'. On 19 April *Australia* proceeded to Sydney, berthing at Cockatoo Island on 22 April and later entering Sutherland Dock for repairs.

While the flagship was *en route* to Australia, events were taking place that must have left Crace in no doubt that the last had not been heard of the convicted stokers. As he noted in his diary, he knew that Rapke was 'very upset & considers that legally they should have been found not guilty'. On 20 April, however, Rapke formally wrote to him to state his concerns over the finding. He pointed out that though Riley's statements implicating the accused and suggesting a strong motive for murder were inadmissable evidence and had been rigorously excluded from the trial, nonetheless 'on joining "Australia", I found that the nature of this evidence was common knowledge in the ship [and] two members of the Court were officers in "Australia"'. Rapke went on to detail other matters which he considered 'insupportable in law' and had contributed to a miscarriage of justice, including the fact that, as prosecutor, Farncomb had made known to the court his own firm personal view that the two men were guilty. He submitted to Crace that the conviction was wrong both in law and in fact, that the court had misdirected itself, and that evidence of identification used in the case was insufficient in law to support the finding.

Farncomb, too, wrote to Crace on 20 April, to make a statement in mitigation of the sentence of death passed on two members of his ship. He acknowledged that such a statement might have been given to the court after the finding of guilty was brought in; 'I was, however, acting as Prosecutor in the case and felt some diffidence in offering to make a statement without adequate consultation with the Accused's Friend.' He now asked for his statement, written in his capacity as commanding officer of the men concerned, to be forwarded with the court martial documents. 'My object is to stress the abnormality of the present times and to draw attention to the probability that this abnormality is likely to produce a warped state of mind in certain men, who in more happy times would be ordinary, decent, well-balanced individuals.'

Farncomb went on to describe the conditions under which ratings on the lower deck, especially engine room ratings, were presently living and working. He referred to the high temperatures and oppressive humidity entailed in operating in the Tropics, and the limited ventilation, especially at night, caused by the need to preserve the watertight integrity of the ship. He also pointed out that long periods had been spent at sea in these monotonous and uncomfortable conditions, with little opportunity for relaxation. Even when in harbour, frequently only limited leave was given because work had to be done in refitting the ship. Thus, he said, there was an absence of the softening influence of the opposite sex, or of contact with practically anyone outside the service. 'Finally the circumstance of the war, in which life seems to be held so cheap, is an especially evil influence.' Farncomb asked that the cumulative effect of more than two years of such conditions on the state of mind of some men be taken into consideration, pointing out that both Gordon and Elias had been in *Australia* since the outbreak of the war. Both had, in fact, been in the navy for more years than this, though both were only aged 24; Gordon was an orphan, and his brother, Lieutenant Frank Gordon RAN, had been killed in February 1942 over Norway serving as an aviator on HMS *Victorious*, while Elias was a widowed mother's only son.

Crace added his voice to this plea by his Flag Captain, and in forwarding this representation stated that he concurred with it. He took the opportunity to respond to some of the matters raised by Rapke, however, and pointed out that in the selection of court members defence objections to two officers from the flagship had been upheld by the court and that Rapke had then made no other objections on this score. Similarly, he noted that Farncomb's appointment as prosecutor had been in accordance with a requirement under King's Regulations and Admiralty Instructions that the captain of the ship to which accused belonged was ordinarily expected to act in this capacity; Rapke's submission that Farncomb 'would unduly influence the Court by virtue of his rank is rebutted by the fact of his appointment being in strict compliance with the Regulations'.

Although the focus shifted from *Australia* once the flagship docked at Sydney and the two convicted men were transferred to Long Bay Gaol on 22 April, the murder case continued to be the centre of extraordinary proceedings. On 27 April, counsel for the prisoners made an application to the High Court of Australia for a writ of habeas corpus or, alternatively, a writ of prohibition, to prevent the death sentence on the men being carried out — the first time such an application had been made in the history of the court. Reserving the right to argue the jurisdiction of the court martial, and whether the proceedings before it amounted to a denial of natural justice, defence lawyers argued that under Section 98 of the Commonwealth Defence Act a court martial had no power to sentence members of the Australian defence forces to death except for mutiny, treason or desertion.

Another strand was added to this line of argument when Rapke asked Crace on 28 April to seek Navy Office confirmation that, by some secret order early in the war, the ships and personnel of the RAN had been placed at the disposal of the British Admiralty for the period of hostilities. A reply was received the same day that, indeed, such a transfer of the Commonwealth's vessels, officers and men to the King's naval forces had been made by an Order-in-Council on 17 November 1939. The fact of this transfer was added to the defence case when the matter came before the Full High Court later the same week. It was contended by lawyers acting for the condemned men that the Governor-General was not entitled to sign the warrant which had authorised Crace to summon the court martial, and that Crace's own jurisdiction to convene a court martial on RAN personnel was tainted by uncertainty whether he did so under the authority of the Australian Naval Board or his RN warrant.

Not until 8 July was the outcome of the appeal known. In a unanimous judgement, the court ruled that the Naval Discipline Act 1866 (Imperial), not the Defence Act 1903–41 (Commonwealth), applied in this case, but that the court martial had been properly constituted and possessed the necessary authority to convict and sentence the stokers. Accepting also that court martial proceedings were not subject to control or revision by civil courts, it dismissed an application for leave to appeal.

The War Cabinet also discussed the case in the wake of the High Court decision and, as Crace had earlier surmised, there was no eagerness to see the two men actually hanged. The Minister for the Navy, Norman Makin, had already been receiving representations about the case, such as that from the Speaker of the New South Wales Legislative Assembly on behalf of the Darling Harbour Branch of the Australian Labor Party, which objected to the death penalty as 'a relic of the barbaric ages', and another from solicitors for Elias' mother, who voiced objections through a federal member of parliament that RAN men had been tried under the rules of the British navy. Ministers evidently felt secure in the belief that the death sentences on Gordon and Elias could not be carried out without the government's consent, and that it was also within their power to commute these sentences to some lesser penalty. Here, however, the Cabinet was brought face to face with a startling fact. Arising from the action of the government in office in 1939 in placing the RAN under Admiralty control, it was now realised that Australia had given away 'all powers of remission, suspension, annulment, modification or confirmation of sentence', according to the Commonwealth Defence Act and Commonwealth Naval Defence Act, in respect of Australian personnel subjected to court martial. Rather belatedly, action was taken to claw back these powers so lightly handed over to Britain.

On 21 July, the Prime Minister's department cabled the Secretary of State for Dominion Affairs in London, asking that 'steps be at once taken . . . to confer upon Governor-General in Council the powers and functions of remissions specified . . . and to make such powers exercisable as to cover two present sentences of death'. The reply to this request was somewhat less than encouraging. The Secretary of State said that the matter was being gone into immediately but that questions were raised which 'may present considerable difficulty'. It would, he said, be possible in the case of the present death sentences to have these remitted by the King, on the advice of the Australian government, under Section 53(1) of the Naval Discipline Act 1866, and he suggested that to avoid delay Australian authorities consider making a submission to the King recommending commutation.

This answer drew a rather sharply worded follow-up cable from the Prime Minister's department on 31 July. London was asked to 'specify the difficulties to which you refer. So far as we can see the legal difficulties are capable of removal by you.' The present complication, it was contended, had only arisen because the Commonwealth Parliament had not yet adopted the 1931 Statute of Westminster, which gave Australia virtual legal independence from Britain. This meant that Australia faced the anomalous situation whereby the Commonwealth retained control over commutation of offences by members of its army and air force, but not its navy. While this general question was being resolved — the Statute of Westminster was ratified later that year — the government nonetheless adopted the other course suggested to it regarding Gordon and Elias. Pointing to the features of the case which justified commutation, the government recommended that the King reduce the death sentences on the two men to life imprisonment. The procedure adopted at the court martial 'was, in some respects, irregular and this was commented upon by one of the Judges who concurred in the decision to refuse the remedy of Habeas Corpus'. Moreover, consideration of the case by responsible ministers would have led the Australian government, if the matter had been in the hands of the Governor-General, to recommend commutation. On 10 August, advice was received from London that the King had agreed to commute the death sentences to life imprisonment.

Despite the success of supporters in having the sentences of the convicted stokers reduced, agitation about the case still continued. Solicitors acting for Elias' mother sought the setting up of a government inquiry as a means of 'clearing up the unsatisfactory features of the matter ... (inter alia) the sufficiency of the evidence on which the two men were convicted'. As a result of these representations the Attorney-General's department actually asked CNS for an opinion as to whether any basis existed for an inquiry. Admiral Royle's reply, conveyed by the Navy department on 26 November, was to the point. There was, he said, no difference in the legal procedure followed in a naval court martial under Australian law or British law and, apart from possible legal technicalities which were already being reviewed by the Attorney-General's department, he was satisfied that the two accused had been given a fair and just trial by a competent court.

Even this did not bring to an end what were described in one Navy department document on 3 December 1942 as the 'extraordinary legal arisings' of the affair. A persistent campaign alleging the innocence of the men, pressed most prominently at this stage by a Sydney woman claiming to be among the 'friends and next of kin' of Gordon but who was well known to naval intelligence and described there as 'a woman of very doubtful character (to say the least)', finally had its effect by December 1943. On 17 December the Attorney-General, Dr Herbert Evatt, wrote to Makin saying that he was continually receiving representations for the reduction or remission of the sentences of Gordon and Elias. 'I do not propose to indicate the nature of the allegations and insinuations that have been made but they are of such a nature that, in the interests of justice, any doubts as to the guilt of otherwise of these men should, in my view, be cleared up at the first convenient opportunity.' Evatt therefore proposed arranging for a judge of a superior court to conduct an *in camera* inquiry into the circumstances of the trial and any alleged miscarriage of justice.

The Attorney-General's proposal was viewed in Navy Office as an extraordinary review mechanism, but provided the resulting inquiry was not simply a transparent attempt to set aside the legitimate procedures of the original court martial the Navy was prepared to cooperate. The judge obtained for the inquiry was Justice Allan Maxwell of the New South Wales Supreme Court; sitting as a commissioner, he held hearings on the case during February 1944. In the report of his findings Maxwell was unequivocal that the decision of the court martial had been perfectly correct: 'I have no doubt at all that the prisoners were guilty as charged,' he wrote, and, agreeing with the description of their crime as a 'brutal and sadistic murder', he could find no reason to recommend that the whole of the sentences be remitted. Maxwell dismissed most of the defects of the trial alleged by counsel for Gordon and Elias, but he did accept that Farncomb's declaration to the court that he personally believed in the guilt of the accused to have been 'a substantial defect'. Though rejecting any suggestion that Farncomb had unfairly tried to influence the tribunal, Maxwell considered that he did fall into error in making his remarks. He concluded that members of the court, or some of them, might well have been unduly influenced by the prosecutor's address, even though there was nothing to indicate that they had been so influenced. In all the circumstances Justice Maxwell considered that grounds existed for remitting some part of the sentences, and he pointed here — ironically — to precisely the factors which Farncomb had set forth in his statement of 20 April. These, the judge argued, would certainly have been taken as mitigating circumstances by a court dealing with the question of setting a term of imprisonment.

While Maxwell found that a partial remission of sentence could be recommended, he did not indicate the extent of any such remission because he believed he was not authorised by the terms of reference for his inquiry to do so. Responding to a subsequent request by Evatt, however, the judge gave his opinion that reduction of the sentences to 12 years imprisonment would be justified. The Naval Board could see no reason why two brutal murderers, having already been spared hanging, should receive a further reduction in sentence. Perhaps members of the Board were mindful of the other victims of the tragedy and of the Navy's obligations to them. At the time of the events on the *Australia*, an official telegram had been sent to Stoker Riley's parents in Tasmania, informing them of their son's death and extending the usual sympathies but stating nothing about the circumstances. It was only after reading an item in a Sydney newspaper on the case that the old couple learnt the awful truth regarding the murder of their only son. A deeply distressed Mrs Riley wrote on 28 May, 'It is the most disgraceful, and tragic, happening that has ever come to my notice.' Although unwilling to see Riley's murderers further favoured, in the circumstances the Naval Board now saw no alternative to accepting Justice Maxwell's recommendations. However, in January 1946, when Elias' mother raised the question of her son receiving the six-month remission of sentence granted all prisoners in commemoration of Allied victory in the war, the Board decided to stipulate that neither prisoner was to receive the benefit of any remissions, for good behaviour or any other reason—they were to serve a full 12 years, as recommended by Justice Maxwell, and instructions were issued to this effect in April of that year.

Even with the substantial remission already won, or perhaps because of this concession having being made, supporters of Gordon and Elias continued to lobby politicians, prominent clergymen, and such groups as the Returned Servicemen's League and the Trades and Labour Council, claiming their innocence. Faced with this continuing interest in the case, in 1949 the Attorney-General's department finally queried whether Maxwell's recommendation had actually meant to exclude further remissions of sentence to which the two former stokers (by now they had been dismissed from the RAN) would normally be entitled within the prison system of New South Wales. This point was raised with the Navy department, and was considered by the Naval Board on 21 December. At this meeting the Board decided that, 'while loath to relax the already reduced punishment for such a crime', it accepted that Maxwell had been misinterpreted and therefore approved the usual remissions applying in the case of these men. With that, Gordon and Elias were released from prison in September 1950.

At the stage which the Pacific War had reached in April 1942, things looked grim indeed for the Allied cause. Japanese forces had been everywhere successful on land, while Allied naval forces had been swept from Asian waters and the Indian Ocean. The Australian mainland itself had been attacked, with heavy bombing of the northern city of Darwin from February, so that invasion of Australia itself seemed likely. On 17 March US General Douglas MacArthur, having escaped from Japanese beseigers in the Philippines, arrived in Australia, and the Australian government handed over to him the operational command of all combat sections of its navy, army and air force.

To control the Allied resistance to the Japanese onslaught, the Pacific theatre had been divided into four major military operational areas—north, central, south, and south-west; there was also a separate south-east area contiguous to the coasts of Central and South America. The first three of the main subdivisions were placed under Admiral Chester Nimitz, Commander-in-Chief of the US Pacific Fleet at Hawaii, who also now became Commander-in-Chief of Pacific Ocean Areas with authority over all Allied armed forces within their boundaries. MacArthur, by mutual agreement between the US, Britain and Australia, was appointed Supreme Commander of the South-West Pacific Area (SWPA), a title he soon changed to Commander-in-Chief to match Nimitz's.

Under these new arrangements, Anzac Area ceased to exist on 22 April; New Zealand now became part of South Pacific Area which, from 8 May, came under the command of Vice-Admiral Robert Ghormley, acting under Nimitz's overall direction. The former Anzac Force became the naval force for SWPA and was promptly dubbed 'MacArthur's Navy'. On the headquarters which MacArthur raised, Vice-Admiral Leary became Commander, Allied Naval Forces, SWPA or COMSOUWESPAC as it was abbreviated. Australia's CNS, Admiral Royle, was designated Commander, South-West Sea Frontiers, under Leary's loose control. Crace remained the senior seagoing commander, but the former Anzac Squadron was reconstituted as Task Force 44, comprising the RAN vessels *Australia* (flagship), *Canberra* and *Hobart*, and the American ships *Chicago* and *Perkins*.

But while these changes were coming into effect, Crace was more excited by word he received that Rear-Admiral Victor Crutchley, who had indeed been appointed as his replacement as RACAS, had sailed on 12 April aboard a ship that would get him at least as far as New Zealand. The entry in his diary said it all: 'Marvellous news.'

6 Into the Coral Sea

B Y March 1942, Japan's strategic planners had begun pondering the courses open to them following the stunningly successful program of conquest waged by their forces over the preceding three months. Having attained the vital object of securing a defensible perimeter around territorial gains made in the Pacific and southern Asia, a range of options was now open. Several of these had been canvassed in the Basic War Plan laid out in Japanese Combined Fleet Operation Order No. 1, promulgated on 5 November 1941. This document identified areas to be 'rapidly occupied or destroyed, as soon as the war situation permitted', including areas of eastern New Guinea, New Britain, Fiji and Samoa; the Aleutian and Midway Atoll areas; areas of the Andaman Islands; and important points in the Australia Area.

Of these courses, the army staff favoured continuing the offensive in the Pacific Islands beyond New Britain, which had already been seized, to include the capture of the major Allied base at Port Moresby, as well as the Solomon Islands, the New Hebrides, New Caledonia, Fiji and Samoa. The purpose of this thrust was to cut the vital line of communication between the US and Australia, thereby isolating Australia and negating its potential as a supplier of fighting personnel and commodities, and a base from which resurgent American military might could be applied against Japan's new possessions. The naval staff, on the other hand, advocated either a direct invasion of Australia or a western advance against India and Ceylon, although the commander of the Combined Fleet, Admiral Isoroku Yamamoto, a brilliant strategic thinker, still nurtured a scheme of his own. With America's greater economic base (and hence its capacity to outstrip Japan's military strength over time) firmly in mind, he urged the bringing on of a decisive naval confrontation in the east, by thrusting against the US territories of Midway and the western Aleutians.

The debate over these conflicting proposals recognised that there were clear limits to Japan's existing military strength. The General Staff of the army opposed the India option, and also the idea of attempting an invasion of Australia. According to the army department's calculations, the latter course would entail using the main strength of the navy, along with the cadre troops of twelve army divisions, requiring about 1.5 million tons of shipping for transport. A new mobilisation of this magnitude could be achieved, it maintained, only by a drastic curtailment of military operations on Japan's fronts in Korea and China. More than this, however, it would adversely effect the nation's overall strategic posture. Planning for the operations already undertaken in the 'Southern Region' had been based on an expectation that the army need for shipping would gradually decrease, thus freeing tonnage to develop mobility within the boundaries of Japan's hugely expanded empire. Rather than the requirement for shipping on this front dropping from the eighth month of war onwards, as planned, to only a million tons (approximately half the tonnage on the national register at the outbreak of war), an invasion of Australia would actually tie up military forces far exceeding the total of all troops so far employed in this region and soak up available shipping. Changing the pre-arranged programme with a new commitment of such magnitude was, in the General Staff's view, 'an extremely irresponsible operation ... [which] would decidedly exceed the limits of Japan's national strength', and the army decided it could never assent to the proposal.

Given this opposition, plans for invading Australia were abandoned in favour of a less ambitious scheme to simply isolate the Australian continent and effectively force it out of the war. While he acquiesced in the army's plans. Yamamoto did not believe that operations in the south-west Pacific would achieve the cherished goal of precipitating a decisive defeat of the US Pacific Fleet. With his staff at Combined Fleet Headquarters at Hashirajima, the admiral continued to urge the necessity of drawing the Americans into a big fleet action and argued that only by threatening Midway and the Aleutians would this be achieved. By early April he had obtained the reluctant consent of the naval staff, although questions of timing and other details remained to be settled. These matters were still unresolved when Tokyo and other Japanese centres came under a reprisal air raid on 18 April from a small force of US army bombers under Lieutenant-Colonel James Doolittle. These aircraft had been secretly taken within range of the Japanese home islands on board a naval force (Task Force 16, comprising the aircraft carriers *Enterprise* and *Hornet*) commanded by Vice-Admiral William Halsey. While the Doolittle Raid produced neglible military results it had profound psychological impact in Tokyo, appearing to confirm the soundness of Yamamoto's analysis of the threat posed to Japanese naval superiority by the continued existence of the American carrier force. Consequently, on 5 May, the Imperial General Staff ordered the Midway operation to be carried out in early June.

While this operation of vital significance was being debated, preparations continued for the southern thrust already decided upon. Overshadowed by the larger argument occurring over the Midway attack, or Operation 'MI' (for Midway) as it was known, arrangements for what was called Operation 'MO' (for Port Moresby) was carried forward with uncharacteristic complacency. There seems little doubt that a mood of elation over Japan's string of easy successes had engendered a contempt for Allied military forces and must be seen as a factor in the Japanese approach to this operation. But the distraction of the Midway debate had also caused the other operation to be viewed in the High Command as a subsidiary activity, so that there was insufficient interest and oversight taken with regard to it.

Planning for Operation 'MO' was left primarily in the hands of the local commander, Vice-Admiral Shigeyoshi Inoue, commander-in-chief of the Fourth Fleet and concurrently commander of the South Seas Force. The principal objectives selected were Tulagi, halfway down the Solomon Islands chain, and Port Moresby. The occupation of these two places had been originally scheduled for March, but was delayed by the appearance of US carrier forces in the area. Now Inoue and his staff at Rabaul, embarked in the light cruiser *Kashima* which had been converted for use as a command vessel, planned an operation in successive moves. Firstly, a forward seaplane base would be established at Tulagi, to cover the flank of the move on Port Moresby and support the subsequent advance towards the south-east. This was to be followed by an amphibious assault on Port Moresby, and seizure of phosphate-rich Nauru and Ocean Islands.

Although relatively straightforward in its aims, the plan devised by Inoue was complex in conception. Involving no fewer than six separate naval groups, it depended on their coordinated movement from widely separate starting points according to a prearranged timetable. Such a scheme presupposed a degree of tactical competence among the commanders which would have been demanding in the best of circumstances, let alone on this occasion when Japanese planning involved a number of important miscalculations. While Inoue assumed that there would be an Allied reaction to his moves, intelligence available to him indicated that opposition would come mainly from US and RAAF aircraft operating from bases in North Queensland, and a 'British' sea force—obviously Crace's Task Force 44—comprising destroyers, a light cruiser, two or three heavy cruisers and a battleship (which presumably *Australia* was taken to be). More importantly, however, it had been assessed that just one US carrier—*Saratoga*—could be deployed to spearhead any attempt to interfere with Inoue's plan. In fact, *Saratoga* was in a dockyard on the American west coast undergoing repairs after a Japanese submarine torpedoed her in January, but there were still two other US carriers available—*Lexington* and *Yorktown*—even discounting the possibility of getting Halsey's Task Force 16, with *Hornet* and *Enterprise*, into the fray following their return from the Doolittle Raid. Also, Inoue did not count on his enemy having significant forewarning of what was afoot, which they did. Due to the American ability to read much of the Japanese naval code, from mid-April Allied intelligence was aware that a large naval force was being assembled at Rabaul for an operation expected to be launched early the next month. Only the precise objectives of this operation remained concealed, although it was guessed that either or both Port Moresby and the north-eastern coast of Australia were targets.

The forces to take part in Operation 'MO' were organised into:

- **Port Moresby Invasion Group**: five navy and six army transports commanded by Rear-Admiral Koso Abe, carrying the 3rd 'Kure' Special Naval Landing Force and the 144th Regiment of the South Seas Force of Major-General Tomitaro Horii*; screened by a squadron of six destroyers, and accompanied by one minelayer and four mine-sweepers;

---

* At full strength the South Seas Force totalled about 5300 men, but this included an engineer regiment, anti-aircraft artillery, and medical and transport detachments, in addition to the three infantry battalions of the 144th Regiment. The 3rd Kure SNLF was a battalion group of about 1200–1500 men, so that—all up—the Port Moresby invasion force probably totalled no more than about 6000 troops.

the whole commanded by Rear-Admiral Sadamichi Kajioka on board the light cruiser *Yubari*;

- **Tulagi Invasion Group**: one transport, one seaplane transport, two destroyers, two submarine chasers, five minesweepers; commanded by Rear-Admiral Kiyohide Shima on the minelayer *Okinoshima*;
- **Support Group**: comprising the seaplane tender *Kamikawa Maru*, two cruisers, three gunboats, and one minelayer; commanded by Rear-Admiral Kuninori Marushige;
- **Covering Group**: light aircraft carrier *Shoho*, four heavy cruisers, one destroyer, one oiler; commanded by Rear-Admiral Aritomo Goto on board the heavy cruiser *Aoba*;
- **Striking Force**: two fleet carriers (*Shokaku* and *Zuikaku*) under command of Rear-Admiral Chuichi Hara in *Zuikaku*, two heavy cruisers, six destroyers, one oiler; commanded by Vice-Admiral Takeo Takagi on board the heavy cruiser *Myoko*;
- **Submarine Force**: a patrol group of five boats, and a raiding group of two boats; commanded by Captain Noboru Ishizaki.

Quite apart from the elaborateness of Inoue's dispositions, these also betrayed what British writer Richard Humble has termed 'a casual allocation of force'. This was most noticeable in respect of the carriers. Only one small carrier with 21 aircraft aboard (12 Zero fighters and nine Kate torpedo bombers) was allocated to providing air cover for both the Tulagi and Moresby landings; on the face of things this was taking very lightly the air defences at the latter place, which on the eve of 'MO' contained some 25 US Airacobra and RAAF Kittyhawk fighters. It was also inescapable that the 12 000 ton *Shoho* was not a front-line vessel. It was actually the remodelled submarine tender *Tsurugizaki* which had completed conversion in December 1941; with a top speed of only 25 knots it was unsuitable to operate with big carriers and had thus been detached from the Combined Fleet for a secondary role with Goto's covering group.

The *Shokaku* and *Zuikaku* could in no way be regarded at inferior units, but they, too, were a telling comment on the attitude with which the Japanese prepared to enter the Coral Sea. Both ships were of the same class: each displaced nearly 26 000 tons, steamed at 34 knots and were capable of carrying 84 aircraft. Launched in 1939, they were, as Humble calls them, 'the fastest and toughest fleet carriers in the Pacific' at that time. But they were just one division of the force of five fast carriers under Vice-Admiral Chuichi Nagumo which was now back from a successful hit-and-run raid on British forces in the Indian Ocean and which could have ensured Inoue's success was complete. As it was, Nagumo's force needed to make good his aircraft losses from recent operations, and the *Zuikaku* and *Shokaku* were assigned to Operation 'MO' as the vessels which could best be spared. Indeed, it is clear that the assignment of units to Inoue's expedition was generally limited by the preparations underway for the forthcoming Midway attack, thus highlighting the folly of the compromise which had been reached over Japan's strategic options.

Ignoring the caution warranted in the circumstances, Inoue settled on a bold scheme which made direct provision for Allied intervention. Assuming that the US carrier force believed to be available to respond would go after an invasion group moving on Moresby from Rabaul, he planned to trap it between the twin prongs of Goto and Takagi. These forces would come south from Truk in the Caroline Islands, and move in conjunction with the invasion transports, thus being on hand to deal with the expected American-Australian counter-move. While the Allied force was being engaged by these powerful groups, Kajioka's transports would make an uninterrupted run into Moresby. Having crushed Allied resistance, Takagi's carriers were then free to hammer with air strikes the key ports and airfields of North Queensland: Horn Island, Cooktown, Coen and Townsville.

As previously noted, much of this was anticipated by the Americans by virtue of their ability to read Japanese signal traffic, and the two carrier task forces which had previously operated in the SWPA were again readied for action. Task Force 17 (or Task Force Fox), with Fletcher on board *Yorktown*, had finished replenishing at Tongatapu and sailed on 27 April. Its frequent crisscrossing of the waters in this area had resulted in the ship being dubbed 'Waltzing Matilda', but this time its return to the Coral Sea promised to be no mere outing. Task Force 11 (Task Force Baker), led by *Lexington*, was already on its way down from Pearl Harbour where it had been refitting, only now it was commanded by Rear-Admiral Aubrey Fitch, one of the US navy's most experienced 'air admirals'. Nimitz had replaced Brown with Fitch on 3 April in deference to King's view that Brown was not aggressive enough to lead combat forces.

Some difficulty was experienced in putting together an adequate force to provide a screen for the two American carriers, and in the event there were just five heavy cruisers available for this purpose (*Minneapolis, New Orleans, Astoria, Chester* and *Portland*), along with nine destroyers (*Phelps, Dewey, Farragut, Aylwin, Monaghan, Morriss, Anderson, Hammann* and *Russell*). So far as aircraft were concerned, broad parity in numbers existed — 146 planes being embarked on the three Japanese carriers while the two US ships carried 151. These numbers were well below the full complement of the carriers, but enabled each ship to accept some at least of another's air group in an emergency.

Nimitz also decided to commit Halsey's Task Force 16. This had arrived back in Hawaii on 25 April and needed some days to replenish, but on 30 April it put to sea and sped south. Halsey was not likely to reach the Coral Sea before 15 May, but Nimitz considered it worthwhile to send him in the hope that the Japanese plan might suffer some delay which might enable his two carriers, four heavy cruisers and eight destroyers to play a useful role, and their presence might well tip the balance in the Allies' favour.

In view of the shortage of ships to screen the US carriers, the availability of the ships of Crace's Task Force 44 was a factor important to the overall equation. At this point, *Chicago* and *Perkins* were at Noumea, while *Australia, Hobart* and *Canberra* were at Sydney — the first two undergoing minor repairs and the *Canberra* refitting. *Hobart* was also in the process of becoming the first RAN vessel fitted with radar, the aerial of the only radar set in Australia being mounted on its foremast on 28 April. *Chicago* and *Perkins* were ordered to a point 320 miles south of San Cristobal Island, where they were to rendezvous with the two carrier groups.

Crace had still been on passage to Sydney for repairs to his flagship when first told by Leary that an extensive Japanese movement southwards from New Britain was expected after 3 May, and he was instructed then to have his ships ready again for sailing by 1 May. The commanding officer of *Hobart*, Captain Harry Howden, had been similarly forewarned before the ship began its repairs in April. A later CNS, Sir Richard Peek, then the cruiser's gunnery officer, recalls that Howden promptly passed the news to the ship's company while steaming down Port Phillip Bay. Taking a risk with security, he announced from the bridge that the six weeks leave due to all ranks would be reduced to two, as he had been told by COMSOUWESPAC that *Hobart* could expect to be in a major battle in the Coral Sea early in May. If anyone spoke of this, Howden said

The light cruiser *Hobart* became the first RAN ship to be fitted with radar just days before leaving Sydney for the Coral Sea. It is shown here wearing the camouflage in which it fought the battle. (*RAN Photographic Unit*)

he expected to be court-martialled, but in the event his show of faith was not misplaced.

As predicted, on 1 May Task Force 44 was ordered by Leary to join up with US forces in the Coral Sea three days later, and *Australia* and *Hobart* accordingly sailed from Sydney; unable to be made ready in time, *Canberra* remained behind. Arriving at Hervey Bay (120 miles north of Brisbane) at 3.44 the following afternoon, the two cruisers rounded Breaksea Spit and anchored in the north-eastern corner of the 40-mile-wide bay. They found already there the RAN ships *Bingera* (an anti-submarine vessel), *Kybra* (tender) and *Kurumba* (auxiliary tanker), the last-named coming alongside soon after they anchored to commence refuelling. Also present was the flush-decker *Whipple*, one of two American destroyers sent there to rendezvous and provide an escort for the Australian cruisers. The other ship, *John D. Edwards*, had developed defects and been forced to return to Sydney.

As soon as fuelling was completed, at 9pm, the two cruisers proceeded to sea in company with *Whipple* and joined up with Task

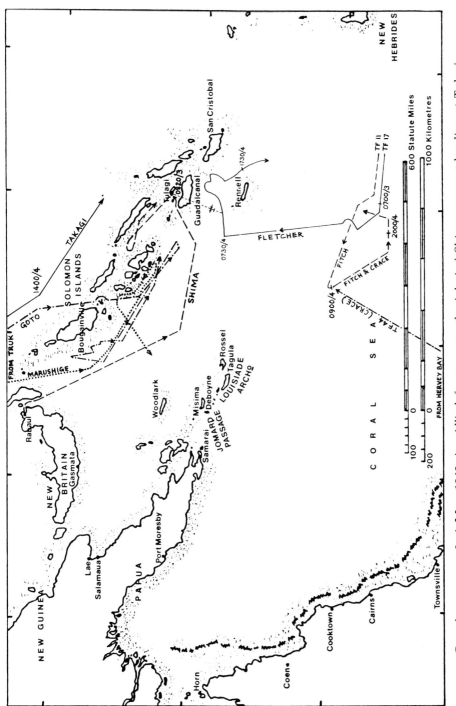

Opening moves, 3–4 May 1942 An Allied force consisting of Admiral Fletcher's Task Force 17 (from Tongatapu), Admiral Fitch's Task Force 11 (from Pearl Harbour) and Admiral Crace's Task Force 44 (from Sydney via Hervey Bay) assemble south; Admiral Shima covers a landing at Tulagi, prompting Fletcher to launch carrier-strikes against this place on 4 May. (*Note:* all dates and times shown according to 24-hour clock, followed by day in month of May.)

Force 11 on the morning of 4 May. Recalls Jack Langrell, a crewman on the *Australia*: 'We were ordered to meet the American task force at 8 a.m. It was a hazy day, but we had an excellent navigator—Commander Rayment—and precisely at 8 o'clock, in the haze, we were right in the midst of the battle fleet.' At this point *Whipple* parted company and steamed away to the south. Shortly after dawn the next day, some 320 miles south of Rennell Island, the combined force was met by *Perkins*, actually one of Crace's ships but which had, along with *Chicago*, been operating with Task Force 17; two hours later, at 8.23am, *Yorktown* and the main body of the other task force were sighted.

Fletcher's group was returning from an operation against Tulagi the previous day. After receiving reports of the unopposed Japanese occupation of that place on 3 May, he had taken Task Force 17 northwards in the expectation of finding plenty of worthwhile targets and intending to inflict maximum loss. But the major enemy units which supported the landing had not stayed after the troops went ashore. Departing three hours later to embark on the next phase of the operation—the seizure of Nauru and Ocean Islands—most of Shima's ships were long gone before Fletcher got within striking distance. Nonetheless, a series of three strikes by Douglas TBD-1 Devastator torpedo-bombers and SBD-2 and SBD-3 Dauntless dive-bombers were made on Tulagi between 8.15am and 3pm on 4 May, the first of these taking the Japanese completely by surprise. As British naval historian Richard Hough describes it:

> The excited air crews observed the shock waves circling out from the blasts, the mixed columns of water and debris, a capsized ship, running figures on shore, the criss-cross pattern of tracer fire: all heady stuff to these navy aviators.

Unfortunately, the results of this action hardly warranted the description 'battle' later applied to it. Only four minor vessels were destroyed (the largest being a destroyer), and three more—including Shima's flagship *Okinoshima*—were damaged. More useful in the circumstances was the destruction of five H6K 'Mavis' aircraft, big four-engine flying boats used for long-distance reconnaissance. 'Hardly an annihilating victory', as Hough observed, but a heartening piece of punishment to have served up to the enemy nonetheless. For once the Japanese were completely at the mercy of their adversaries; though the garrison commander sent radio appeals for support, there was none close at hand. The American carrier planes had the skies over Tulagi to themselves and lost just three of their number to groundfire (with the pilots of two of these subsequently rescued).

At this stage Crace's squadron came under the orders of Admiral Fletcher. Though he was actually senior to Fletcher, there was never any question of the Australian naval commander taking control of this combined force. While the Coral Sea lay within MacArthur's SWPA, not Nimitz's theatre, the combined Chiefs of Staff Committee — the supreme body coordinating the British and American war effort from Washington — had decreed in March that the senior US naval officer commanding a carrier task force was, regardless of relative rank, authorised to exercise tactical command of combined units operating in the South and South-West Pacific areas. This edict ensured that elements of the Pacific Fleet which might enter SWPA remained under Nimitz, not MacArthur. As the senior of the two US carrier force commanders, this placed Fletcher at the head of the attempt to break up the Japanese move, using hit-and-run tactics as the only means open to him.

As it happened, Admiral King in Washington harboured considerable unease about Fletcher's suitability for the task at hand. At a three-day conference with Nimitz in San Francisco beginning on 25 April, King expressed his concern that Fletcher was possibly insufficiently aggressive for the sort of operation expected of him. Nimitz shared some of this doubt, but the two commanders — recognising that unless Halsey reached the Coral Sea in time there was little that could be done about it — decided to wait and see how Fletcher performed. The implication of this was, however, clear: as Halsey was the Pacific Fleet's most successful carrier commander, it was Nimitz's intention to have him take charge of the operations of the combined carrier groups once he arrived. Unfortunately for this intention, Task Force 16 was still 1000 miles distant when the expected collision of forces took place.

The 21 ships of Fletcher, Fitch and Crace cruised in company in bright sunshine throughout 5 May, the 'dazzle' camouflage of the Australian cruisers distinguishing them from the US ships painted plain blue-grey. During the day, fuelling of the combined force was begun from the fleet oiler *Neosho*, one of a new class of big fuel tankers built for the US Navy from 1938; commissioned in August 1939, the *Neosho* was 553 feet long and displaced 25 000 tons. At 7am on 6 May Fletcher formally integrated all the various warships under his command into the single Task Force Fox, and 30 minutes later brought into effect a reorganisation. Under this, Crace was given command of the force's support group consisting of the cruisers *Australia, Chicago* and *Hobart* and destroyers *Perkins* and *Walke* (a recent addition to the force). In the account of the Coral Sea written by Bernard Millot, Crace's selection was viewed as both 'a gesture to Admiral Crace's personal bravery, ... [and] a diplomatic act of courtesy to Australia and her grim determination to fight off any invader'. More likely, Crace would have wondered whether this signified the impending relegation of his squadron to the sidelines yet again. That afternoon Crace's ships were still waiting for their turn to refuel when many reports of enemy units to the north led Fletcher to stop fuelling operations and to send the *Neosho* off southwards with its destroyer escort (*Sims*) to the next fuelling rendezvous.

By this stage the Japanese operation was in full swing. Already Kajioka's transports bound for Moresby had departed Rabaul and were headed south. Moving parallel to them was Goto's force, which had previously covered the Tulagi landing and then swung across westwards to do the same for the Moresby group. Further east still was Takagi's striking force, moving down the eastern side of the Solomons; this latter group entered the Coral Sea round San Cristobal at the southern tip of the island chain on the night of 5 May, and was thus poised to take in the rear any Allied forces sent to intercept the transports. Already to the south of Woodlark Island was Marushige's support force, bound for Deboyne Island in the Louisiade Archipelago where it was to set up a temporary seaplane base.

Under the divided command arrangements which prevailed, Fletcher was largely dependent on intelligence provided to him from MacArthur's resources. These included Australia-based aircraft of the US Army Air Force and the RAAF. A task group of 11 submarines based at Brisbane was also patrolling the northern Coral Sea, although this—like the Japanese submarines deployed—would make little contribution to the coming action. A chain of Australian coastwatchers across the islands also formed an important intelligence network, but in this case did not come into the picture to any extent because of the location of the Japanese naval concentrations and movement. From MacArthur's sources Fletcher obtained some valuable and timely information, including that which had enabled his opportune strike at Tulagi. At the same time, much of this reporting was of limited use or—worse—down-

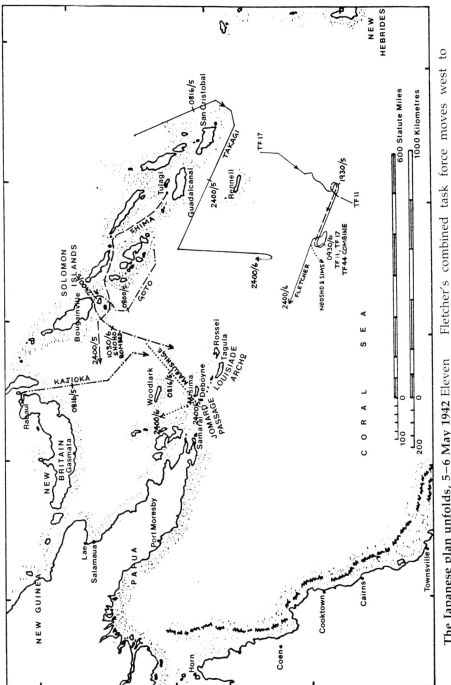

The Japanese plan unfolds, 5–6 May 1942 Eleven transports carrying the invasion force of about 6000 troops bound for Port Moresby sail from Rabaul under Admiral Kajioka, covered and sup- Fletcher's combined task force moves west to intercept, while a powerful striking group under Admiral Takagi moves in from the east to catch the Allied fleet in the rear.

right misleading. A shortage of high speed long range planes and the fact that Moresby was the sole advanced air base available to them posed major problems for the reconnaissance efforts of the shore-based air forces. Not only were there gaps in the coverage achieved (for example, Kajioka's convoy was able to leave Rabaul without being immediately detected) but Allied aircraft were forced to operate at the limits of their range, making it impossible to engage in long searches or trail targets once sighted. Added to these drawbacks was the inadequacy of information provided by aircrews poorly trained in ship recognition.

Faulty data of this sort not only presented a problem for the Allied naval force attempting to steer its way towards the enemy, but also limited the capacity of shore-based strike aircraft to contribute to the breaking-up of the Japanese movements. On 4 May Allied reconnaissance found the *Shoho*, the light carrier in Goto's covering force, which from now and until after the battle was wrongly identified by Allied intelligence as *Ryukaku*. It was then located south of Bougainville, but attempts to keep the vessel under surveillance were not successful. Although there were a number of reported sightings of an aircraft carrier during 4–6 May, some of which might possibly have correctly referred to the *Shoho*'s position, the others were presumably phantoms. When *Shoho* was picked up again on 6 May *en route* for Misima Island, an attempt was made to strike at it by a flight of three B-17 Fortress bombers of the US 19th Heavy Bombardment Group in Queensland. This attack missed the carrier by generous margins, allowing its commander time to launch fighters to chase the Americans away. If lack of skill on the part of MacArthur's air elements was a frustration for Fletcher, the other side of this coin was that land-based air squadrons operated throughout this time in total ignorance of the whereabouts of friendly ships, which were maintaining rigorous radio silence, and were not even aware that a major naval engagement was being fought until after it was over!

Initial advice reaching Fletcher regarding Japanese movements was, accordingly, thoroughly confusing. Reports indicated there were more than 50 enemy vessels in the New Britain-Solomon Islands area, but pointed to the presence of practically every type of ship imaginable. Included were either one or two aircraft carriers, a battleship (considered doubtful), seven cruisers, 18 destroyers, a submarine tender and six submarines, a seaplane carrier, as well as 17 troop transports and merchantmen. (This estimate was not far wide of the real situation.) While it was thought probable that some vessels had already arrived at Deboyne Island to support an advanced seaplane base, the remainder of the enemy units appeared scattered and no common direction of movement could be discerned.

Only by late afternoon of 6 May did Fletcher gain a clear idea that the invasion force was headed in a direction that would take it through the Jomard Passage, in the Louisiades off the southern tip of Papua, on 7 or 8 May. It was at this point that he suspended fuelling and immediately set course north-west to effect an interception, pushing his force's speed up to 25 knots. What he did not know was that Takagi was then only 70 miles due north himself engaged in fuelling his striking force. Neither side had aerial patrols out, and so both failed to discover the other's presence. Had they done so, a major naval engagement must surely have followed then instead of two days later. As it was, Takagi reversed course and moved away to the north until the early hours of the following morning, when he again tracked south planning to resume the search for the US carriers with the coming of daylight.

At 6 am on 7 May Fletcher had reached a point about 130 miles due south of Rossel Island. On receipt of further reports from Hawaii and Melbourne regarding Japanese movements, he was now also aware that the force covering the transports bound for Moresby was in the proximity of Misima Island. The fact that a carrier (not identified but actually the *Shoho*) was reported to be part of this force led him to deduce that this was where he would find the main carrier force known to be participating in the Japanese operation. At 6.08 am he issued instructions for Crace and his support group (now designated Task Group 17.3 and with the American destroyer *Farragut* added to it) to proceed on the same north-westerly course, while he himself turned northwards. Crace was to cover the southern exit from the Jomard Passage and attack and break up the invasion group as it emerged to begin its approach towards Moresby, leaving Fletcher free to move on where he understood the Japanese carriers to be.

Shortly before 7 am, this separation took place. An hour later Crace sent an information signal to the six ships of his squadron giving them his own estimate of the situation, based on the same intelligence reports reaching Fletcher. There was, he considered, a minimum enemy strength between Bougainville Island and the Louisiade Archipelago of '6 cruisers, 1 Aircraft Carrier, 1 Sea-plane

Carrier, 15 destroyers, 17 transports and merchant ships, 3 submarines and some auxiliaries'. Most units appeared to be concentrating about Deboyne Island, he said, but one report 'indicates some units proceeding to Jomard Passage. Our carriers will no doubt attack today and we are proceeding to destroy enemy units which may pass through Jomard.' With that Task Group 17.3 continued the dash to intercept the invasion group in what became known as 'Crace's Chase'.

Crace had not proceeded very far when his position was detected by a Japanese reconnaissance aircraft and reported back to Rabaul. At about this time Admiral Inoue also learnt of Fletcher's location from Goto, who had located the US carriers and was preparing an attack by the *Shoho*. Sure that his plan to trap the American force between the pincers of Goto in the west and Takagi in the east was about to bear fruit, Inoue focussed his attention on sweeping aside Crace's ships using shore-based attack aircraft despatched from Rabaul. While ever this enemy presence threatened to bar the exit from the Jomard Passage he was unwilling to expose the troop transports bound for Moresby, and accordingly at 9 am he ordered the invasion group to turn about for the time being, at least until Crace had been eliminated.

Meanwhile Takagi, apparently unknown to Inoue, had been diverted from his purpose of closing in on the American carriers from the east, having to contend with some of the same problems as his foes. Receiving a report from a scout that an enemy carrier and a cruiser had been spotted 350 miles south-west of Rennell Island, Takagi accepted that this indicated that the main Allied force had been located. He accordingly closed distance on the target while his air commander, Hara, prepared to launch an all-out bombing and torpedo attack. As it happened, however, the ships about to be engaged were not American carriers at all, but Fletcher's detached oiler *Neosho*, which because of its odd-looking upperworks had been mistaken for a carrier, and its escorting destroyer, *Sims*.

When the Japanese strike force, led by Lieutenant-Commander Kakuichi Takahashi, a veteran of successive carrier actions since Pearl Harbour, including Darwin, arrived over the luckless US ships to discover that the full weight of the carriers had been sent against a target which, while valuable in itself, was nowhere as important as the opposing carriers, he was presented with the

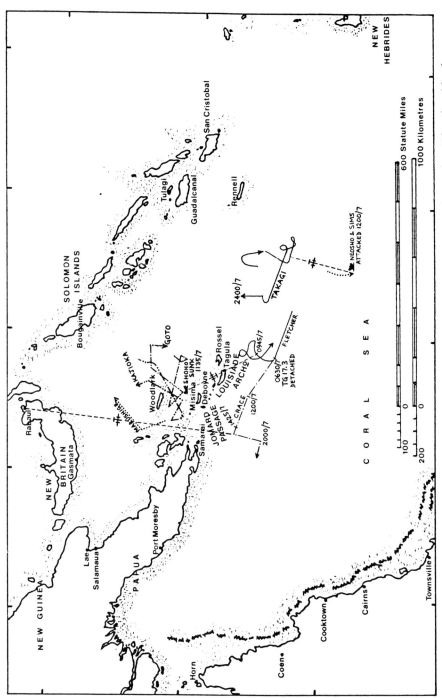

First blows traded, 7 May 1942 Fletcher detaches Crace's squadron to ensure interception of the enemy transports while he launches a strike which results in the destruction of the Japanese ... Shoho south of Misima meanwhile Takagi wastes crucial time sinking the US oiler *Neosho* and its escort *Sims*; that afternoon Crace, by now south of Jomard Passage, comes under attack from Rabaul-based bombers.

dilemma of what to do next. Maintaining a search with part of his force in case the sought-after carriers were nearby, he sent the rest of his aircraft to destroy the two targets he presently had. The result of this division of forces was what one naval historian has described as an 'uncharacteristically inept affair', which took two-and-a-half hours to sink the US ships and in all diverted Takagi for five precious hours from his main task of locating and attacking Fletcher.

In part, this outcome was the result of the fierce defence put up by the *Sims*. After repelling the bombing efforts of a single enemy plane at 9am, the destroyer was patrolling about a mile ahead of *Neosho* a half-hour later when the two ships were the focus of attention for another 15 high-level bombers. These failed to hit their targets, as did another 10 aircraft which appeared at 10.38 and made a horizontal attack in which all their bombs were dropped simultaneously. Swinging hard to starboard, the *Sims* skipped away from their point of impact. About noon, however, 36 dive-bombers came onto the scene, attacking from astern in three waves, and the ships' luck finally ran out. *Sims* sustained three hits from 500-pound bombs in quick succession, two of these exploding in its engine room. A survivor later stated, 'She seemed to split up the keel and just disappeared.' Sinking stern first, it took with it the lives of 379 men; only 14 of its crew survived.

The *Neosho* also suffered from the bombers, sustaining seven direct hits and eight near-misses within a few minutes. It took the impact of a Japanese aircraft suiciding against its No.4 gun station to finally disable the tanker. Blazing fuel from the crashed plane's ruptured tanks flowed along its decks. The captain gave the order to 'make preparations to abandon ship and stand by', an instruction which many of the crew took to mean the ship was finished. These men jumped over the side and took to the life rafts; they were only found ten days later, by which time just four of 68 men in the rafts were still alive. In fact, the *Neosho* did not sink. Its partially empty tanks kept it afloat despite a list of 25 degrees. Those who stayed with the hulk as it drifted north-west towards the Queensland coast were rescued on 11 May by the destroyer USS *Henley*; 123 survivors were taken off the wreck before it was scuttled.

Fletcher, meanwhile, had his own scouts out hunting for the main Japanese carriers to his north (they were actually east of him). At 8.15am one of *Yorktown*'s aircraft reported that it had found two carriers with four cruisers 175 miles to the north-west, in the northern approach to the Jomard Passage. Understandably, this information led Fletcher to believe that he had found the prize he was after. He accordingly dashed forward, preparing to deliver a heavy strike by his carriers against it. A combined attack group of 93 aircraft was in the air by 11am and on its way to deal what Fletcher hoped would be a shattering blow. His dismay can be imagined when the scout plane landed soon after the despatch of the strike force, and it was learnt that a coding error by the aircraft's crew had caused a sighting of two cruisers and two destroyers to be misreported. A full-dress attack by the US carriers had been wasted on a target of purely secondary value, in the same way and at the same time as Takagi was squandering his strength on *Neosho* and *Sims*.

Faced with the alternative of recalling the attack groups in the air or letting them proceed in the hope that they might yet find some worthwhile targets, Fletcher decided on the latter course and was rewarded in his gamble. On course to the location originally reported for the two enemy carriers, an American airman chanced to sight the *Shoho* with its escorts 25–30 miles to starboard and the mass of planes turned to the attack. Concentrating on the carrier, they quickly overwhelmed the hapless ship. Three planes making the first pass failed to hit it, though a near-miss blew aircraft overboard from the flight-deck. There was small chance of the *Shoho* escaping however, and following aircraft quickly scored two direct hits with 1000-pound bombs which crippled its steering gear and brought the ship to a dead stop. Now still in the water and on fire, it was a sitting target, and in the 15 minutes which followed it was smothered with a further 11 bomb and seven torpedo hits. At around 11.35 it sank, taking with it all but about 100 of its complement of over 700. In addition to the aircraft that went down with the ship, several of the Japanese carrier's aircraft were also shot down, so that just three of its planes survived the attack.

Fletcher had achieved a significant success for the loss of just three of his own planes. The short-lived career of the *Shoho* made it only the second carrier in history sunk by another carrier (the first was HMS *Hermes*, a victim of Nagumo's carriers off Ceylon in April) and the first Japanese carrier lost to American action in the war. Even so, it still left Fletcher at a disadvantage to Inoue, who knew his position while that of Takagi's carriers remained unknown to him. By early that afternoon, the US attack groups had been recovered, refuelled and rearmed, and were ready to fly off again.

Briefly Fletcher contemplated a second strike against the *Shoho*'s cruiser consorts but decided these targets were not worth the risk. In any event, the previously perfect weather was beginning to turn, making flying conditions less favourable.

7 Crace's Chase

MEANWHILE, 7 May was also proving to be (as Crace described it in a letter to Admiral Royle) 'a very thrilling day and a mighty lucky one for Task Force 44'. Closed up at action stations and maintaining speed at 25 knots, Crace aimed to arrive off the Jomard Passage about 2pm, thus allowing five hours of daylight to make contact with the enemy transports as they attempted to pass through. He realised he would be mainly reliant on shore-based and carrier aircraft for further information, the risk to his squadron being too great to attempt the launch and recovery of the aircraft borne in the cruisers.

Radar indicated considerable aircraft movement in proximity to the group, but rarely were any of these planes even glimpsed and Crace was initially inclined to think that the odds were still with him that his whereabouts were unknown to the enemy. He was, however, very conscious of the air threat to his squadron, which was absolutely without air cover. Based on the latest air reconnaissance reports, at 10am his revised assessment of enemy strength was that there was a carrier north-east of Pocklington Reef (abot 250 miles north-west of his own position) and another carrier with nearly 30 other warships and transports off Misima Island (about 120 miles north). The carrier off Misima in particular posed an air menace which Crace was anxious to avoid closing too rapidly. He therefore took the precaution of adopting anti-aircraft formation, the cruisers forming a diamond with *Hobart* and *Chicago* respectively each eight cables (1600 yards) on *Australia*'s port and starboard quarters, with a screen in front formed by a destroyer stationed six cables (1200 yards) ahead of each cruiser—*Walke* to port, *Perkins* leading *Australia*, and *Farragut* to starboard.

At 11.30am an aircraft was spotted shadowing the ships and Crace now had to assume that his presence was known to the

Japanese, even though there continued to be no significant sightings of aircraft well into the afternoon. In fact, as previously noted, his force had actually been found by the enemy before it had gone very far at all after separating from Fletcher. A twin-float monoplane from the base established at Deboyne Island by the *Kamikawa Maru* sighted the group soon after 8.00am and had been constantly shadowing it out of gun range ever since. This aircraft reported back to Rabaul that the Allied squadron it was tracking included two battleships, a heavy cruiser and four destroyers, a mistaken claim which had some highly significant results. Admiral Inoue could not help but be alarmed by the presence of such a significant enemy force in such an inconvenient spot for his operation. While the contingency of an American carrier presence had been adequately provided for in planning, as he still believed before the loss of the *Shoho* upset the equation, he could not ignore Crace's apparent intention to place himself astride the route of the Moresby-bound transports. Accordingly, aircraft of Rear-Admiral Sadayoshi Yamada's 25th Air Flotilla took off from Rabaul to deal with Crace's task group.

Meanwhile, the ships of Crace's group remained generally unaware of developments with the rest of the Allied force, though radio transmissions monitored on the frequency used by US carrier aircraft indicated that Fletcher was engaged and enjoying success. When a pilot was heard reporting that they had 'got the Carrier good', this was correctly assumed to refer to the Japanese carrier with the large force off Misima and Crace felt great relief that the air threat to himself had thus been considerably lessened.

Shortly before 2.30pm, when Task Group 17.3 was about 70 miles south of Deboyne, a little west of Jomard Passage, eleven aircraft were sighted at long range to the south. These approached from the stern, travelling on the same westerly course as the squadron, but failed to correctly identify themselves if they were Allied planes. Several ships accordingly opened fire on them as they flew past on the port side, but Crace noted that they were 'low and out of range', and they turned away and passed out of sight. The precise identity of these planes seemed open to doubt. Although taken to be hostile, descriptions indicated that they were probably US Martin B-26 Marauder land-based twin-engine medium bombers. The likelihood that they were friendly was heightened when, some ten minutes later, a Dauntless dive-bomber from an American carrier approached *Australia*, correctly identifying itself. Recalls

Leading Signalman Mervyn Johnston, who was on afternoon watch on the bridge of the flagship, a repeated request was received from this plane by voice radio, 'Where are the carriers?' As this information was unknown to the task group, Johnston says that Captain Farncomb ordered that the Dauntless be given the bearing and distance to Port Moresby: 'This was repeated to the plane by signal light several times when it suddenly disappeared as quickly as it had come.'

The squadron continued as before, closed up at first degree of readiness which meant personnel were at their action stations. Recalls Jack Langrell on the flagship:

> Nothing was happening to us, although the battle was raging 2–300 miles away. It was a hot day and we were given permission to go on the upper deck to get some fresh air, but told not to go far from our battle station. I was on the mess deck and went up the hatch behind A Turret [mounting the ship's forward pair of 8-inch guns] and sat down there enjoying the afternoon.

Shortly before 3pm, a formation of aircraft was detected on radar at a distance of about 75 miles. At 3.06 these planes came into view with the sun behind them, bunched together two or three miles off the port bow. There could be no doubting their hostile intent, as they approached at only 50–100 feet above the waves—a sure indicator of impending torpedo attack. They were, in fact, twin-engine land-based bombers from the 25th Air Flotilla at Rabaul, though accounts are confused as to the number and type involved. Various Allied versions claim there were between eight and eighteen planes, usually stating that these were Mitsubishi Ki-21 Sally medium bombers, though some refer to the presence of Zero fighters too.

The account of Japan's naval air force during the war by Masatake Okumiya and Jiro Horikoshi states, however, that 44 aircraft took off from Rabaul to strike at Crace, these comprising 33 Mitsubishi G3M Nell bombers (a navy type very similar in appearance to the army's Sally, the main difference being in the tail) and an escort of 11 Zeros. In fact, Okumiya states that the 25th Air Flotilla included only Nell bombers on its strength, so that the question of type of bomber involved seems to be effectively settled. Fighters would, of course, have taken no part in such an attack, but remained on patrol above to intercept any Allied planes which might arrive to disrupt the bombers' work.

This photo, taken from USS *Chicago*, shows the opening moments of the air attack on Crace's Task Group 17.3 on 7 May 1942. HMAS *Australia*, preceded by USS *Perkins*, commences to hurl defensive fire against approaching Japanese torpedo bombers. (*IWM neg.56165*)

As the disposition of a large number of the bomber force which reportedly left Rabaul can be accounted for from later events, the evidence suggests that the force first seen bearing in on Task Group 17.3 consisted of twelve to fourteen Nells. This certainly confirms Crace's own estimate that twelve bombers took part, but does not reconcile with Okumiya's claim that 'twenty of the twin-engined bombers carried torpedoes, the remainder, bombs'. The best that can be made of this is the apparent confirmation that the bombers were all of one type, and the possibility that Okumiya may have reversed in error the numbers fitted with the different armaments.

Crace altered his squadron's course to bring the approaching aircraft head on as they rapidly closed distance, then ordered his captains to take independent action. Each ship began radical manoeuvres—altering course in violent zigzags—as fire was opened on the attackers. Crace recalled in his diary that everything was thrown up at them 'except [*Australia*'s] 8-inch barrage & I don't know why that didn't go'. According to Roger Moag, then a gunnery petty officer with his action station in the after director control tower, the reason for this was—incredibly—that, at this very moment, the guns were being unloaded. He says that, as the squadron had been anticipating a surface action, the flagship's main armament was loaded with semi-armour piercing rounds (the normal ammunition for use against ships) and now had to be reloaded with high-explosive for engaging air targets. However, Lieutenant (later Commodore) Allen Dollard, then the forward director for the guns, cannot recall there being any order to unload, which was a cumbersome process requiring crewmen going onto the deck outside the turret and using extractor poles to push the rounds back out the breech. Clearly this was not the moment to be attempting such a procedure. Instead, Dollard is certain that the command 'Barrage, barrage, barrage' had been given — the signal for the guns to be cleared by firing whatever rounds were already loaded — but why this did not happen still remains a mystery.

Ed Znosko, a crewman on the *Chicago*, states that the American cruiser certainly cleared its 8-inch main armament by firing salvoes at the oncoming planes, the big projectiles striking the surface of the sea and throwing up gigantic walls of water as obstacles to the low-flying attackers. More than 40 years later, Znosko also still vividly remembers the sensations of the moment:

> I scrambled through the escape hatch to man my battle station as a stretcher-bearer in the after-battle dressing station, located in the stern of the ship in the Chief Petty Officers quarters. The 5-inch anti-aircraft guns could be heard in rapid fire, and the ship was shaking and vibrating from the full speed on our four large propellers and frequent changing of course to dodge Japanese torpedoes. On reaching my battle station I suddenly became scared and had to urinate, but I was trembling so much facing the urinal that I could do nothing.

In his post-action report Crace wrote: 'The bombers never faltered and came on through a very intense fire. One of the centre ones leading was hit (by *Perkins* I think), burst into a huge flame and crashed, and the rest started dropping their torpedoes.' Johnston also recalls this moment, stating: 'The USS *Chicago* opened fire first and hit the leading Japanese plane which at the same time as it exploded dropped an orange or yellow flare of some sort. This apparently was the signal for the following bombers to drop their torpedoes.'

The weight of the anti-aircraft barrage had the effect of causing the attackers to release their torpedoes almost bow on, and at the relatively long distance of 1000–1500 yards. The *Australia* found itself in the path of two torpedoes sent racing towards it. Wrote Crace:

The view from HMAS *Hobart* as the task group claims its first attacker, which lies burning on the water's surface. The US destroyer *Walke* is screening in front of the Australian light cruiser. (*Cdre D. H. D. Smyth*)

> The day was calm and sunny and the sea very blue so that the tracks were very easily seen. How those torpedoes were avoided beats me and I could have laid very long odds that two on the starboard side must hit. They can only have missed by a matter of feet. Farncomb handled the ship extremely well and it was entirely due to him and a great deal of luck that *Australia* was not hit.

Others on the bridge of the flagship also testify to the narrow margin by which torpedoes passed alongside, although not surprisingly in such a fast-moving action recollections varied slightly, depending on where different observers were standing or looking at particular moments. Lieutenant Charles Savage, also stationed on the bridge during the attack, saw the wake of one torpedo ahead pass close down the starboard side as the ship sharply turned: 'Everyone was waiting for the bang which didn't come as we passed over the wake of the torpedo, which fortunately is some distance ahead of the water disturbance . . . Similarly the wake of one other passed close across the stern.'

At least eight torpedoes were counted as having been loosed against the cruisers — three aimed at *Australia*, one at *Hobart*, and four at *Chicago*. These had produced close shaves for other than just the flagship. *Hobart*'s war diary refers to the torpedo aimed at it having passed close along its port side, and — as the figures show — the US cruiser had been no less a focus of enemy attention than the flagship, at one stage reportedly having three torpedoes converging on it. According to Crace, two aircraft had attempted to get within close range of it, during which the torpedo from one plane actually passed underneath *Chicago*. But due to skilful handling by all the ship's captains, and the heavy fire thrown up by the defenders, the squadron had so far sustained no direct hits and escaped any serious damage.

Not that the ships were totally unscathed. After releasing their torpedoes, the bombers had continued to fly straight on at the ships, strafing with machine gun and cannon fire as they came. Bill O'Sullivan, a member of an aft gun crew on *Hobart*, saw one aircraft flash by at deck height, 'as large as life a stone's throw away' with the pilot's face clearly visible through the perspex hood of the cockpit. An observer on the bridge of the *Australia* also recalled: 'It was warm work. It seemed to take us some time . . . to realise that the odd buzzing noises about our ears were in fact, machine gun bullets!' Johnston, too, was momentarily fascinated at being able to see the pilots in the planes as they went past, but seeing them firing and hearing the bullets he dropped down onto the deck.

For Jack Langrell, still quietly enjoying the afternoon air behind A Turret when the attack began, these few minutes had been a nasty jolt. In his own words:

> All of a sudden all hell broke loose so I quite realised then this was definitely the Japs coming in. I turned around to go down the hatch I'd come up, only to find it was securely locked. I was caught on the upper deck, so I just stood behind the turret. One of the Japanese torpedo bombers would have been 100 feet from the ship's side and level with the upper deck as it passed down the port side. Unbeknown to me they were spraying the ship with machine-gun bullets.

Standing on the compass platform, Crace also was unaware of the strafing and watched the bombers pass by without taking cover:

Dramatic pictures as the Japanese attack develops. *Above* Bombers
(circled) dart among the Allied warships, braving the anti-aircraft
barrage. (*IWM neg.HU56166*) *Below* One torpedo bomber veers in to
make an attack, while another lies burning on the water at right. (*IWM
neg.HU56167*) These photographs are possibly taken from movie
coverage of the attack filmed from *Chicago*, and the ship's wake in the
foreground is probably that of the flagship *Australia*.

After dropping their torpedoes the Japanese bombers flew on
directly at the ships of the task group to strafe them with machine-
gun fire. This scene, recorded by a seaman aboard *Hobart* using a
box camera, shows the *Australia* being passed by one attacker while
another crashes in her wake. Visible beyond the flagship's bow is
USS *Perkins*. (*Cdre D. H. D. Smyth*)

> The planes then came roaring past each side within fifty yards
> range and below bridge level if anything. I know they seemed to
> be below me. I did not see any machine gunning as they passed us
> and certainly no one was touched forward . . . I am kicking myself
> now for not having noticed more details of the machines etc. as I
> had a marvellous view with nothing to do to distract my attention.

In fact, there were nine casualties among the crews of the task
group as a result of the strafing attacks. Six of these were RAN
men—three on *Australia* and three on *Hobart* (including its commanding officer, Captain Howden, who received a flesh wound in
the arm from fragments caused when one of the ship's light anti-
aircraft guns fired into the shield of another gun).* All the Australians recovered from their injuries, but of the three American

* Apart from Howden, the casualties on the *Hobart* were AB J. P. Hickey, and OD J. C.
  Whittle. The wounded on the *Australia* were AB G. A. Best, AB R. P. Tolley, and OD
  H. E. Clayton.

casualties, two ratings from *Chicago* named R. E. Reilly and A. B. Shirley subsequently died. Reilly, one of the ship's bakers, was hit in the head at his action station (manning a 36-inch searchlight on the mainmast) by the fire from a tail-gunner in one passing bomber; recalling that he was stretcher-bearer and had to lower Reilly from the searchlight platform, Znosko commented, 'I never knew why he was manning a searchlight in broad daylight.' Seaman Shirley, wounded at a 5-inch anti-aircraft gun post, also later died of his injuries. The bodies of the two were buried at sea the next day, the presence of the brother of one of them who was serving on board the same ship making this a particularly sorrowful occasion.

The Japanese also suffered losses during their strafing attacks. As Roy Scrivener, then manning a twin mount (double-barrel) 4-inch anti-aircraft gun on *Hobart*, later observed, 'They simply had to, when one realises just how many shells and bullets must have been in the air, fired in the direction of the attackers.' In fact, the fusillade sent up from the ships placed not just the attacking Japanese in peril. Scrivener acknowledges that some of the Allied casualties were very likely caused by the cross-fire of the ships themselves; certainly a sailor aboard the *Chicago* recorded in his diary that the US cruiser had 'shot a hole in *Hobart*'s stack'. In the wake of the battle, a board of inquiry would also be held on *Chicago* to examine evidence that the American cruiser had been hit by stray fire from the Australian ships.*

Already nicknamed 'The Flaming Angel', *Hobart* lived up to its label on this occasion. Following the ship's experience of air attack in the Mediterranean and more recently in action in the Java Sea in February, its gunnery officer, Lieutenant Peek, had mounted additional anti-aircraft weapons 'wherever space could be found' on board, although he admits that 'regrettably little consideration was given to safety firing arcs or blast effect on people manning the guns'. It was, in fact, one of a pair of these added-on weapons installed just forward of the compass platform which provided

---

* As *Hobart*'s gunnery officer, Lieutenant Richard Peek appeared before the board with the approval of his commanding officer and expressed the opinion that such an occurrence was almost inevitable in the circumstances. At this point the US naval officer heading the inquiry ordered these remarks expunged from the record, explaining that although Peek's candour was appreciated and everyone present knew the truth of his statements, it was not desired to give any cause for congressmen in Washington reading the board's findings to make ill-informed and critical observations regarding the ability of the Allies to operate together effectively.

Captain Howden with his wound. *Hobart*'s barrage also had another unwanted effect; it was discovered that every time the 6-inch main armament was fired the ship's radar system was blacked out.

Despite the problems and risks, *Hobart*'s gunners mounted a vigorous defence of their ship. A four-barrelled pom-pom reportedly blasted one attacker to pieces, and a few minutes later another gun crew sent a second enemy machine in flames into the sea, described by Scrivener:

> As one was banking away from *Hobart*, and turning to pass over our port quarter, a direct hit, claimed by our port 4-inch gun blew the aircraft apart. The explosion was felt by those in exposed positions, the heat being extreme. It was assumed, at the time, that the plane's torpedo could not have been released.

While unaware of these successes claimed by members of the ship's crew, Peek vividly recalls 'the one that got away'—a Japanese bomber which, having just dropped its torpedo, banked away in a tight turn which left it momentarily suspended in mid-air only 200–300 yards off *Hobart*'s port side, fully exposed to a four-barrel .5-inch gun mounted there. This easy target went begging, however, when the gun failed to fire, and Peek was sent to find out why. The leading seaman in charge was brought before Captain Howden, still nursing his bleeding arm, and admitted to having left the safety catch on; he was demoted on the spot.

Australia also had success. Crace recorded that one aircraft, passing close in on *Australia*'s port beam, was just in the act of launching its torpedo at *Chicago* when he saw it hit in the tail by an Oerlikon firing from the flagship and crash. In all, at least five of the Japanese bombers were claimed to have been shot down, although some accounts claim that records of the 25th Air Flotilla later showed that ten aircraft had failed to return.

After a furious action lasting just four or five minutes, the surviving torpedo bombers departed. Although brief, the attack had been—in Crace's judgement—'most determined' but 'fortunately badly delivered', in that the attacking aircraft initially 'came from the bow only and . . . in one wave'. No sooner had this attack ended, however, than more bombers appeared at 3.13, approaching from astern and up sun at about 18 000 feet. *Hobart*'s published history records that sweating gun crews had not even had sufficient time from the previous attack to kick the heaps of expended cartridge cases overboard. Johnston, by this stage at his action

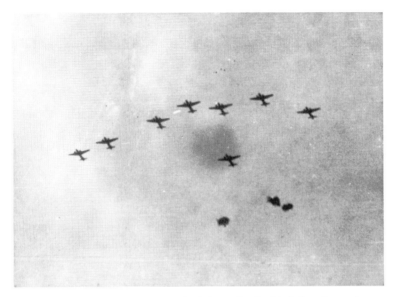

Part of the formation of bombers which launched a high-level attack on *Australia* minutes after the Japanese torpedo-attack ended. From the silhouettes, these appear to be Mitsubishi G3M Nell aircraft of the Japanese 25th Air Flotilla at Rabaul. (*Mr T. M. Johnston*)

station on the Flag Deck, had his attention drawn to these new planes by a companion's remark, 'Gawd, look up there.' He looked to see 'row after row of large bombers coming right overhead. At that precise moment down came the bombs . . . ' In Crace's words:

> We were all congratulating ourselves on a marvellous escape from the T.Bs when all of a sudden up above in perfect formation against the blue sky were nineteen silvery H. L. B.'s [high level bombers]. Almost as I saw them I saw the bombs drop and again Farncomb did the right thing and put the wheel hard a Starboard. The ship had just started to swing and list when down whistled the bombs all around us and all on the Compass Platform crouched down . . . I think most fell on the port bow and starboard quarter so that we should have bought it good and hearty if the wheel hadn't come over when it did.

The attackers' high-level pattern attack was certainly accurate. *Australia* found itself in the centre of the impact square formed by some twenty 500-pound and other smaller bombs, and was per-

A heart-stopping moment, captured on film from the deck of *Hobart*, as Japanese bombs begin bursting around the *Australia*. The columns of water thrown up by the blasts have not yet reached their full height! Visible beyond the flagship are US destroyers *Perkins* (at left) and *Farragut*. (*Cdre D. H. D. Smyth*)

fectly straddled in all directions. Gigantic columns of salt water were thrown up all around it. From *Perkins* the flagship was 'completely blotted out by splashes higher than her masthead'. Other accounts speak of it being completely obscured from view for more than a minute due to spray! Crace was later told by Captain Bode of the *Chicago* that *Australia* was visible in a narrow lane between 'huge splashes almost touching'; the story circulated at the time that Bode saluted the spot where the heavy cruiser disappeared from view and said 'Goodbye, *Australia!*' The Officer of the Watch on the *Australia* remembered that: 'The weight of that water, as it came down over us on the Bridge, and we were 52 feet above the waterline, was sufficient to force us to our knees.' Crace himself was remembered, standing on the bridge, his face and immaculate white uniform now drenched with water, blackened by smoke and stained by the explosive content of the bombs. But although the ship's upper deck was 'soused' (as Crace himself later termed it)

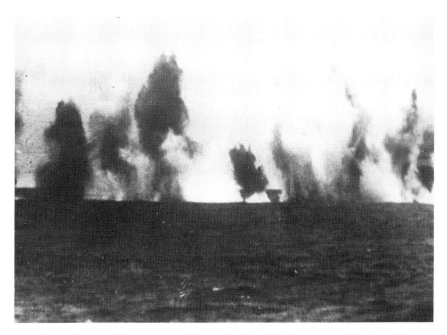

Graphic photos of the pattern of bursting bombs that narrowly missed HMAS *Australia*, causing it to totally vanish from view behind walls of water. The flagship was reportedly obscured completely for more than a minute by spray. (*Top Mr T. M. Johnston; bottom IWM neg.HU56172*)

103

and bomb fragments flew on board there was only superficial damage and no further casualties.

Those on the *Australia* understandably felt they were lucky to have survived this moment, though to some on the *Hobart* it seemed that the flagship had been in no great danger. As one officer of this consort observes, 'Having seen a lot of high-level bombing in the Java Sea, this seemed all a bit ordinary.' While it was true that high-level attacks at sea against nimble high-speed vessels had generally had a low record of success to that time, on this occasion the torpedo attack had successfully diverted attention from the high-altitude approach of the further bombers and almost enabled them to catch the *Australia* napping. Clearly only Farncomb's swift action saved the ship.

For crewmen working on the upper decks of the flagship through successive torpedo and bombing attacks, these events could seem quite thrilling despite an element of fear. The experience was rather different for those enclosed below deck, denied visual knowledge of what was occurring and only able to follow the sounds of battle. For Midshipman Dacre Smyth, two days past his nineteenth birthday, what could be heard was far from reassuring. Writing three days later to his mother, widow of General Sir Nevill Smyth VC, he described the feeling of being shut into his action station in the Transmitting Station, 'listening to the guns, shaken by the bombs, and wondering if there was any chance of any of us getting out from down there if the ship *did* cop it'.

For Cliff Hemming, a ship's cook whose action station was in the confines of the cordite handling room serving *Australia*'s forward 8-inch gun turrets, the experience was very similar. He remembers:

> The cordite was contained in metal boxes stacked to the deckhead above and held in place with hardwood battens. Between us and the ship's side were water tanks, and below us, fuel oil. We were not allowed to wear shoes with nails, etc., as a spark could open up the whole ship. During the Japanese bombing attack, the shrapnel hitting the ship's side sounded like chains dragging across a steel plate. The explosions of the bombs also loosened a few rivets so that water and oil began to seep in, and in our sand shoes we were skating along the deck.

The final episode to this brief but frantic action followed a few minutes later, at 3.19, when three more aircraft came in from the south-west at about 25 000 feet and dropped a salvo of bombs which struck the water some 800 yards ahead of *Australia*. These bombs were evidently aimed at *Farragut* but narrowly missed *Perkins* instead. On the flagship Farncomb ordered the 8-inch guns in the forward turrets to be elevated and opened fire, but without scoring any hits. Johnston remembers remarking then to his companion on the Flag Deck that the aircraft looked to him like friendly planes. Others around him thought the same, and Savage recalls: 'Immediately after their pass at the squadron... the ship picked up intercept [indicating] that the attack had been carried out by US army aircraft who were reporting to Townsville, [claiming] that considerable damage had been inflicted on a Japanese naval squadron.' Much more would be heard of this occurrence following the discovery that they actually were US Army Air Force B-17 Fortress heavy bombers.

With the attackers gone, Crace now had time to reflect on his situation. He pondered the possibility that the aircraft which had flown past his squadron an hour earlier, and were thought to have been 'friendly', were in fact the same ones which began the attack a half-hour later—a line of thought which ignored the range limitations which would have prevented these aircraft spending such a time seeking out targets. It appeared probable to him that the torpedo bombers, and the bombers which followed, 'had been searching for our carriers which had been attacking enemy ships during the day and that having failed to find them, they turned their attention on us'. If this was the case, then Crace felt 'some good had been achieved' although he also considered that it 'showed again the danger of operating surface vessels in the vicinity of shore-based aircraft without any fighter protection'.

Crace faced a difficult decision as to what now to do. The most worrisome aspect for him was the fact that he knew nothing of the whereabouts or intentions of Fletcher and the main Task Force. In the absence of any contact with enemy ships, and with the receipt of reconnaissance reports that the large enemy force previously sighted off Misima was now moving away to the north-west, he could only deduce that the Japanese threat on Port Moresby had been averted, at least temporarily. Since he was without any news of Fletcher, Crace decided to head south until dark and then turn westward so as to continue to provide a blocking force against any Japanese move towards Moresby.

The retirement of the Task Group was shadowed until 6pm by a big Mavis four-engine flying boat presumed to be from the temporary seaplane base at Deboyne Island, occasional sightings of it being made by the ships. This presence ensured everyone remained acutely conscious of the ongoing high air threat and anticipating more air attacks. Midshipman Smyth frankly admitted in his letter home that 'we were pretty jittery', and even Crace admitted that he was 'mighty glad when night came'. In fact, the squadron was spared further enemy attention, though not because of the losses it had inflicted on its attackers earlier in the day.

As Commander Okumiya recorded in his account, the pilots who returned from the attack reported sinking an American *California*-type battleship (presumably *Chicago*), causing serious damage to a British *Warspite*-type battleship (presumably *Australia*), and leaving a cruiser in flames. He was astounded to learn only after the war that no such results had been achieved, and attributed the discrepancies of this 'reporting episode' to two causes. Firstly, he pointed to the fact that the targets were 'highly evasive cruisers and destroyers, which often confused the crews of the attacking bombers', and secondly he claimed that the 'pilots and crews participating in this particular attack lacked combat experience, and their efficiency ranged far below that of the crews which sank the *Prince of Wales* and *Repulse* [in December 1941], and the *Langley* [in February 1942]'. The air units which attacked Crace's squadron were, he states 'manned by hastily recruited replacements' for the veteran air crews lost in February during the futile attack on the *Lexington* when that carrier attempted to raid Rabaul. 'Replacements had come in slowly,' he says, 'the men lacked training, and crew coordination was greatly in need of improvement.'

The effect of the misinformation contained in the reports of returning pilots was that identified by Millot, who remarks that:

> ... the Japanese commanders at Rabaul took these reports at their face value and so failed to launch any further air attacks, since they considered that this Allied force had been annihilated. It certainly could not have been the few losses they had sustained which caused the Japanese naval commanders to leave this Allied force alone.

Around 6.30pm, the prospect of further air attack receding with the approach of evening, confusing reports were received from the Area Combined Headquarters (ACH) at Townsville and from COMSOUWESPAC (Leary's headquarters in Melbourne). These stated, firstly, the presence of five transports, and later three transports and three warships, in Crace's vicinity. As Crace later observed, these reports 'caused doubt for a time as to what the situation really was':

> On that first report I debated whether or not I should close the supposed transports at once and attack at night hoping I should get clear enough by daylight to avoid attack by shore based aircraft. It was only by stretching my imagination to the limit and accepting the possibility that the transports were in fact T. F.44 that I gave up the idea, and then I felt it was hardly justified. Moreover, if there happened to be two task forces within reasonable distance of each other and neither knowing the position of the other (as on the 7th) a very awkward situation might arise involving one attacking the other at night.

This realisation that the reported enemy forces did not exist but were actually his own squadron was most fortunate because, as Crace noted: 'An attempt to intercept may have resulted in serious damage from the air to our group the following day'.

Crace continued to feel anxiety about the absence of information from the main Task Force. Radio transmissions between *Lexington* and *Yorktown* and their operating aircraft had been monitored during the day, but these provided no knowledge of the carriers' whereabouts because of the code being employed, which used a system of referring to positions by letters unknown to anyone in his squadron. Crace was thus in the dark as to what had been achieved during the day or what Fletcher's intentions might be. He expressed his concern about his squadron's vulnerability in a signal addressed to COMSOUWESPAC and Fletcher in the expectation, as he later explained, that the latter, 'who was assumed to be moderately close to the Eastward, would send an aircraft at daylight the following day to inform me of his position and intentions'.

In the meantime he steamed on southward, his ships closed up for a night surface action, and by midnight was about 120 miles south of Samarai. He maintained a westerly course into the next few hours until he heard that the enemy invasion group had definitely turned back to the north. By dawn the next day he was about 220 miles south-east of Port Moresby, in a position from which he could continue to intercept any force moving through China Strait or Jomard Passage but which lessened his exposure to the enemy air threat.

8 *The main event*

DESPITE the significant success supposedly achieved against Crace, by mid-afternoon on 7 May the overall situation in the Coral Sea evinced some distinctly unsatisfactory features from the Japanese point of view. Inoue had been forced to hold back the transports because of Task Group 17.3 but, although he imagined he could now instruct them to resume course following reports of the destruction of this force, *Shoho* had been sunk — thereby depriving him of both the key unit of the invasion's covering force and the western pincer in his plan to entrap the US carriers, which still posed a considerable threat. He knew by this time of Takagi's sinking of *Neosho* and *Sims*, but any satisfaction at this success was dulled by the knowledge that vital hours in which to bring Fletcher's carriers to battle had been lost by this diversion.

Takagi and Hara felt their blunder no less than Inoue, and the failure to find and retaliate against the big American ships for the destruction of *Shoho* involved great loss of pride throughout the striking force. Determined to erase this mistake, and to eliminate Fletcher before he could further upset the Japanese plan, Hara decided on a bold bid to find and attack the US carriers before nightfall. Selecting pilots most experienced in night operations, he launched 12 Val dive-bombers and 15 Kate torpedo-planes shortly before 4.30 pm and sent them off under Lieutenant-Commander Takahashi with orders to attack at dusk when light conditions would hamper the anti-aircraft gunners on the American ships. Takahashi flew a westerly course, towards Crace's position earlier in the day, as some sighting reports from here had mistakenly referred to the presence of carriers and Fletcher was accordingly expected to be found in this vicinity. Since the pilots of the carrier division's Zero fighters were untrained in night operations, they remained behind and the strike force proceeded without fighter escort. As a gamble this effort deserved more success than it achieved. In fact, the 27 planes of the strike force passed fairly close to the US ships they were seeking, but fortune was against them.

Fletcher had also contemplated sending off a further search that afternoon but was dissuaded by the adverse weather. A cold front had arrived during the day and extended east-to-west across the Coral Sea. Conditions encountered by the US force were extremely poor, as noted by Stanley Johnston, a journalist with the *Chicago Tribune* then serving as war correspondent on board *Lexington*: 'We got rain squalls, low scud, and some fog. Visibility was at times zero, and at others lifted to only several miles — tricky flying weather in which carrier pilots work hard and run the risk of losing their carrier.' Fletcher realised that any aircraft sent off at that time of day would have to be recovered on board in conditions of half-gloom caused by the overcast and that stragglers would probably be forced to return in darkness. Since US carrier air crews were not trained for night operations at this stage of the war, this was a prospect he did not relish. He had therefore abandoned this option, preferring to use the cold front for concealment and rely on Mac-Arthur's shore-based aircraft to locate the Japanese carriers for him, and to ensure he was ready to engage the next day.

The wisdom of Fletcher's choice over Hara's was all too apparent to Takahashi's strike force, battling westward through intermittent rain squalls and towering cloud formations. Not surprisingly they failed to sight the Americans, who were shielded by low cloud cover and thus invisible to aircraft lacking radar such as the Japanese. Reaching the limits of their safe range without sighting anything, Takahashi's planes jettisoned their bombs and torpedoes and headed back for their own carriers. Unfortunately their return course brought them close to the very force they had been seeking. Picked up on ships' radar, combat aircraft were vectored out by this means to intercept, and Takahashi's formation suddenly found itself under furious attack in the half-light from Grumman F-4F Wildcat fighters. Eight of the Kates and a Val were shot down, for the loss of just two American planes (one of them piloted by an Australian named Les Knox, formerly of Brisbane).

With the sun having set some 45 minutes earlier and darkness now falling, the Wildcats were recalled to be taken back on board their carriers. Events now took a bizarre twist, as the survivors of

Takahashi's group laid a course for home which took them directly over the top of *Yorktown*; several of the aircraft, mistaking the American carrier for their own, joined the queue of planes preparing to touch down on its flight deck. The Japanese crews, hunting for their parent ships at the end of a long and gruelling operation, had fallen 'victim to the delusions and "mirages" brought on by exhaustion', as Okumiya recounts:

> Several times the pilots, despairing of their position over the sea, 'sighted' a friendly aircraft-carrier. Finally a carrier was sighted, and the remaining eighteen bombers switched on their signal and blinker lights as they swung into their approach and landing pattern.

After some initial puzzlement, the presence of intruders among the circling planes was quickly realised on board the carrier. An American pilot who twigged to the significance of the strange navigation lights on aircraft in front of him was the first to open fire. Lines of tracer-fire from this plane alerted the escorting destroyers which immediately joined in. The Japanese aircraft extinguished their lights and rapidly made off, three of them zooming across the bows of the carrier. Twenty minutes later there was a repeat of this episode when another three bombers attempted to join the landing pattern and were driven off — this time with one of their number shot down. The feelings of the Japanese airmen at these incredible events can be readily appreciated, having endured so much to find the enemy carrier and then to stumble upon the prize when they had already discarded their armaments. On the American side there was some bemused speculation about the situation which might have developed if the Japanese had been allowed to land.

Hara, by this stage desperate to recover his precious planes, took the extraordinary and highly dangerous step of ordering the searchlights of his ships switched on, and played on the clouds to provide a beacon to guide the strike force in. Just six made it back (including Takahashi), their fuel gauges nudging empty. The remaining 11 failed to make the distance, or 'splashed' trying to make a night landing on the carriers. Hara's bold gamble now held the appearance of another fiasco, capping a day of ignominious failure. Instead of getting in a crippling evening blow that might have left the Americans at their mercy to finish off the following day, the

Japanese had merely added to this first day's tally of losses among their own aircrew — in fact, 17 per cent of aircraft strength aboard the Japanese carriers had been lost, all for the sake of an oiler and a destroyer.

Of one thing, however, both sides were now quite sure: there could be no doubting the proximity of the opposing carrier forces. Those of Takahashi's pilots who made it back reported the US presence only 50–60 miles away. For the Americans' part, the radar on *Lexington* at 7.30pm had noted aircraft milling in what was taken to be a landing circle only some 30 miles to the east, indicating the presence of enemy carriers. Due to a handling error, this information did not reach Fletcher on *Yorktown* for nearly two-and-a-half hours, by which time it was practically valueless. Fletcher was sceptical about the report in any event, as no corroborative sighting had come from *Yorktown*'s radar, but given the lapse he had to take into account the fact that the Japanese ships had ample time to have moved a considerable distance. (At that moment they were actually about 95 miles away to the east.) Still, he accepted that the main enemy force was probably within striking distance of himself and that the next day would bring on the much-awaited clash.

In fact, both commanders seriously considered not waiting for the next day but going after each other in night surface attacks. Fletcher ultimately rejected the idea of detaching a force of cruisers and destroyers for this purpose because of the situation he expected to face at daylight with his anti-aircraft screen for the carriers already somewhat thin. Inoue actually issued orders for the cruisers of Goto's covering force and the destroyer screen of the transports of the Moresby invasion force to rendezvous east of Rossel Island and make a night attack on Allied forces, which were unspecified but presumably referred to Fletcher rather than Crace (who was thought to have been destroyed). He reconsidered this plan, however, and by midnight issued new orders postponing the Moresby invasion by two days and splitting Goto's covering force between Takagi and the transports. Takagi, too, weighed the prospects for a night attack, but was forestalled by a plea from Rear-Admiral Abe, commanding the invasion force, for more air protection while his ships made their way back to Rabaul. With the sinking of the *Shoho* there was now considerable nervousness about the transports' vulnerability to attacks from Allied land-based aircraft. This request was met by Takagi turning north, a course which opened distance between his force and Fletcher's, which was then steaming southeast.

While Inoue's orders for the Moresby invasion force to turn back in the final hours of 7 May apparently negated the primary Japanese objective and fulfilled that of the Allies, it was plain that all that had been achieved by this stage was a stay-of-execution for Port Moresby. So long as the invasion force remained intact, the thrust for Moresby could be resumed just as soon as the opposing Allied naval forces had been dealt with. Inoue therefore needed to deliver a blow sufficiently damaging to prevent Fletcher further interfering in his plans. Equally, for Fletcher, only by inflicting maximum damage on the enemy's main battle units could the temporary reprieve which had been won by Crace be converted into solid victory. Thus the scene was set for a clash with an outcome all-important to both sides. If the clashes of 7 May had been, in boxing terms, preliminary bouts, the next day promised to provide the main event.

Looking back at the situation shaping up for 8 May 1942, the metaphor of a boxing match comes repeatedly to mind. Richard Hough recounts the atmosphere on board the *Yorktown* that night, with squadron commanders striving to bolster the spirits of pilots who knew they faced the certain prospect of combat on the morrow. Among these officers he specially mentions Lieutenant John J. ('Jo-Jo') Powers, 'an Irishman from Brooklyn with a broken nose to mark his record as a boxing champion at the Navy Academy . . . [and] already a bit of a legend, respected and admired by his young pilots'.

From daybreak on 8 May scouts from both carrier forces were sent on patrol. At 8.20 am Fletcher had a report of an enemy formation of two carriers, in company with cruisers and destroyers, located about 170 miles north-east of his own position and steaming south at high speed. Two minutes later a interception of an enemy radio transmission made clear that the Japanese had sighted Task Force 17 at practically the same moment. Hoping to get in an early knock-out, Fletcher was first to throw his punch. He handed over tactical command of the task force to Fitch as commander of the air group, and by 9am the first attack formations were taking off from the American carriers.

Groups from *Yorktown* were first away — 24 dive-bombers carrying 1000-pound bombs, accompanied by two fighters, followed by

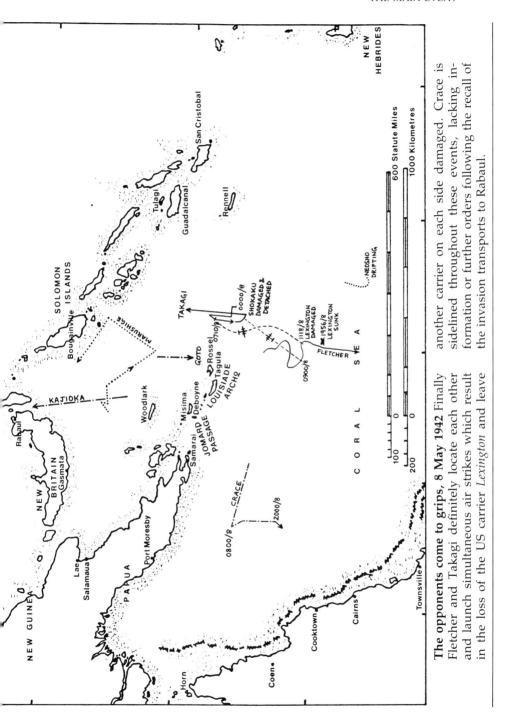

The opponents come to grips, 8 May 1942 Finally Fletcher and Takagi definitely locate each other and launch simultaneous air strikes which result in the loss of the US carrier *Lexington* and leave another carrier on each side damaged. Crace is sidelined throughout these events, lacking information or further orders following the recall of the invasion transports to Rabaul.

nine torpedo-bombers with four fighters. Ten minutes behind came the groups from *Lexington* totalling 22 dive-bombers, 12 torpedo-bombers and nine fighters. Although the carriers they left were in bright sunshine, those they were seeking still enjoyed the shelter of clouds and squalls. The first wave of Dauntless dive-bombers none-theless found the quarry at 10.30am and took cover in cloud to await the arrival of the slower TBD-1 Devastator torpedo-bombers. The two enemy carriers were directly east of Rossel Island, steam-ing south-west about eight miles apart and screened by accompany-ing cruisers and destroyers.

The distance between *Zuikaku* and *Shokaku* at least gave the American airmen one advantage, in that they were free to concen-trate on one carrier at a time without being subjected to the combined fire of both. But Hara was quick to exploit the advantage the weather had granted him. Anticipating what was to come, he took his flagship *Zuikaku* and its escorting group into the convenient cover of a heavy rain squall. *Shokaku*, which was engaged in launching aircraft, was left to bear alone the brunt of the US attack which commenced at 10.57.

Although the *Yorktown* groups coordinated their approach well, their success was disappointing. In making their attack runs the fact that the Devastator was an obsolete type was graphically demon-strated, presaging the disastrous performance of these planes a month later at Midway. (On this latter occasion 36 out of 41 TBDs were lost, causing one historian to observe that the Devastator had become a devastatee.) For the present it became apparent that the requirement for the TBDs to close to 1000 yards at 80-foot altitude and no more than 80 knots (148 kmh) before launching their torpedoes was virtual suicide, as numerous planes were simply blown to pieces by Japanese anti-aircraft fire. In addition, it was discovered again that many of the torpedoes themselves seemed to have faulty steering mechanisms and went looping off in aimless circles once launched.

While the torpedo-bombers failed to register any hits on the

The Japanese carrier *Shokaku* under attack from American carrier planes on 8 May 1942. Even while the US aircraft were inflicting the damage which would force the carrier's retirement from the battle, a Japanese air group from *Shokaku* and sister ship *Zuikaku* was speeding towards the American carriers. (*AWM neg.148953*)

Shokaku, the dive-bombers had more success by lobbing two bombs onto the carrier. The first of these hits was scored by Jo-Jo Powers. He was so determined not to miss that he withheld releasing his bomb until at point-blank range, in the full knowledge that there was no chance of himself surviving the resulting blast, and in doing so earned a posthumous Medal of Honour. His bomb hit the flight deck forward on the starboard bow — 'a straight right hook as he might have recounted if he had lived', as Hough comments — and started a fuel fire. The second bomb landed aft, destroying the engine repair workshop. Thus when Hara reemerged from his sheltering storm a short while later it was to find *Zuikaku*'s sister ship furiously ablaze. *Shokaku* could no longer launch aircraft, though still able to recover them.

The *Yorktown* aircraft broke off the attack at about 11.15 to return to their carrier, their place being taken by the planes from *Lexington*. Regrettably, the majority of the dive-bombing group from this ship failed to locate the target, and it was left to just 15 planes (11 torpedo-bombers and four dive-bombers) to continue the attack. The efforts of the TBDs were again without result, but another direct bomb hit was scored on the starboard side of the bridge. This caused little damage, but the *Shokaku* was by now in serious difficulties anyway and had lost nearly 150 men killed and wounded.

While this struggle was being fought out over the Japanese force, Fletcher was expecting to come in for similar treatment. Like two boxers launching simultaneous punches which land practically at the same time, the enemy air fleet was even then racing south in his direction, having virtually passed his own on its way north. In preparation for this onslaught, the American carriers cleared for action. Fighter patrols were put in constant rotation over the force, with eight Wildcats aloft at any one time while an equal number refuelled on board to ensure all had maximum loads when the moment for combat came. The Task Force was in circular formation, the cruisers forming an inner defensive ring about one-and-a-half miles from the carriers with the destroyers forming an outer ring a further half-mile away. *Yorktown* was about two miles off *Lexington*'s starboard beam. Everytime *Lexington* launched or took aboard aircraft it made a left turn into the wind, frequently straying outside the screen on the port side while its escorts maintained position and disregarded the big ship's manoeuvres.

At 10.55 radar detected the approaching force of enemy planes at a distance of 68 miles. Radioman Vane Bennett on the *Yorktown* later remarked of this sighting, 'It was one heck of a pip. It covered about an inch of our five-inch scope, so I knew it meant an awful lot of planes, spread out deep.' In fact there was 69 aircraft: 18 torpedo-bombers, 33 dive-bombers and 18 fighters — only a few less in total than had been sent against the Japanese carriers. According to Okumiya, a Kate torpedo-bomber flown by Flight Warrant Officer Kenzo Kanno had been shadowing the American ships since first discovering them earlier in the morning. This plane had actually turned for home, having reached its safe fuel limit, when the Japanese attack groups were sighted on their way to the target. Suddenly alarmed that the American ships might still be missed at this distance, Kanno promptly turned around and guided Takahashi's aircraft in — despite leaving himself with insufficient fuel to allow his own return.

Fletcher pushed his ships' speed up to 30 knots and hurried to get off every remaining aircraft on deck. The American effort to intercept the attacking planes was in vain, the Wildcats being too few in number and effectively wrong-footed to make any difference. Fourteen Dauntless dive-bombers which had been part of the early morning scouting effort and were now back with the carriers were also sent up to add to the air defence, though they were ill-equipped for such a role. By 11.16 the enemy planes were upon the US task force and a desperate battle was joined.

Stanley Johnston, watching the action from the signal bridge of the *Lexington*, recorded that the big carrier had not quite regained its position within the fleet formation after launching the last of its aircraft when the Japanese attack force hit. Approaching the big carrier from behind the single cruiser which was then on its port side, instead of the several escorts which should normally have been protecting that flank, the first wave of nine planes came in so low that several of them had to rise to pass over the cruiser. According to Johnston's graphic running account, in doing so 'one disintegrates in the air, simply disappears as if snatched away by some giant magician. Evidently it has been struck by one of the cruisers's heavier shells which also exploded the torpedo.'

Despite strenuous efforts to take evasive action, the giant bulk of the *Lexington* meant it had a wide turning circle of nearly 2000 yards. Planes were thus quickly in position off both bows and dropped torpedoes before flying straight on to zoom over the top of the ship. Johnston recounts the destruction wrought by the carrier's anti-aircraft guns on these attackers:

A dramatic moment during the attack on the American carriers on 8 May, after a Japanese aircraft attempted a suicide crash onto the flight deck of the *Lexington*. Deck-crew watch as the aircraft crashes into the sea after colliding with the tail of the US dive-bomber behind them. (*US National Archives*)

The forward 1.1 battery has the range on that first Jap. I see their shells, bright crimson tracers, tearing through the wings and fuselage. This plane wavers, begins a slow roll to its left and veers off just enough to pass in an inverted position just under our bow. As it glides by I see flames coming from the tail, and the machine smashes itself into the water 50 feet off our starboard bow.

The port forward 5-inch battery manned by Marines concentrates its fire on the second Jap. As this plane zooms to cross almost directly over these guns, they hit it squarely with a shell. The explosion blows it to bits, its engine plunging into the water almost at the foot of the battery. Shreds of its wings and tail surfaces slither along the carrier's deck like sheets of paper swept in front of a gale . . .

The combat taking place looked no better from the viewpoint of the Japanese pilots engaged, with Lieutenant-Commander Shigekazu Shimazaki from the *Zuikaku* later describing his experience to Okumiya in the following terms:

When we attacked the enemy carriers we ran into a virtual wall of anti-aircraft fire; the carriers and their supporting ships blackened the sky with exploding shells and tracers. It seemed impossible that we could survive our bombing and torpedo runs through such incredible defences . . . I had to fly directly above the waves to escape the enemy shells and tracers. In fact, when I turned away from the carrier, I was so low that I almost struck the bow of the ship, for I was flying below the level of the flight deck. I could see the crewmen on the ship staring at my plane as it rushed by.

Notwithstanding the ferocity of the carrier's defence, it sustained a hit at around 11.20; recorded Johnston, 'The *Lexington* shudders under our feet, and a heavy blast spouts mingled flame and water on our port side forward. A torpedo explosion, and we can see the wakes of others streaking towards us. These missiles dropped by those first eight Japs are only just now reaching us.' Moments later the carrier was shaken by a second torpedo also striking on the port side opposite the bridge, sending up another 'spout of flame enclosed in water'. Almost immediately the ship came under attack from dive-bombers plummeting from 17 000 feet to release their bombs at just 2500 feet. A hit was sustained from a bomb landing on the port forward gun gallery, hitting a ready ammunition locker just outside the admiral's cabin and destroying three 5-inch guns located there in an explosion which killed most of the marine crews manning them. Two near misses on the port side which immediately followed were initially mistaken for torpedo hits. A further bomb then hit the gig boat pocket of the port side, before yet another strike was sustained on the smokestack structure, causing more casualties among personnel stationed on the catwalk as it exploded inside. Widespread fires resulted, and as well the colossal 'whip' effect from the blasts of these hits and near misses distorted the hull and buckled plates. Adding to the din of battle was the ship's siren which was damaged and became jammed, wailing weirdly until the last of the Japanese aircraft had departed and the opportunity could be taken to cut off the steam powering it.

The *Yorktown*, meanwhile, had weathered the Japanese assault in somewhat better shape than its companion carrier. Being smaller, it was more manoeuvrable (its turning circle was only half that of 'Lady Lex') and this had enabled its captain to successfully dodge nine torpedoes. The ship was still unscathed when the dive-bombers started their work at 11.24. Several near misses were experienced as their 800-pound missiles were evaded, but one finally hit it at 11.27. This struck the flight deck, 15 feet inboard of the island and about six feet to starboard of the centre line, penetrating the flight, gallery, main second, and third decks before exploding in a storeroom three feet above the fourth deck. Although 37 men were killed in the blast, and another 30 were badly injured, mainly with burns, the overall effect of this hit was minimal. Fires which broke out were quickly controlled, and the ship suffered no great structural damage but was able to maintain speed above 24 knots. Flying operations were also still able to continue.

The Japanese attack ended at around 11.40, just 24 minutes after it had begun. The whole of the long-awaited carrier-versus-carrier clash lasted 43 minutes from the time the first US planes swooped on the *Shokaku*. Fletcher was now able to assess his situation. The *Lexington* was obviously the more seriously damaged, having developed a list of about six degrees to port and having both flight-deck elevators jammed — fortunately in the up position. Its state seemed far from irretrievable, however, as its engines were unaffected and continued steaming at 25 knots. Within an hour damage control was able to report that three fires had been extinguished, a fourth was being contained, and the list was corrected by shifting oil ballast. Flying operations were resumed, with the carrier able to accept back on board its returning aircraft. It appeared to have survived the attack with combat effectiveness unimpaired.

Fletcher nonetheless decided against launching a second air strike, influenced by the fact that he had lost 33 aircraft and others were now unserviceable. He also decided against closing the enemy main force for a surface engagement, considering that he did not know the extent of the damage the Japanese carriers had suffered. Pilot reports suggested that *Shokaku* had been sunk and *Zuikaku* damaged, but there was no confirming this at the present time. Consequently Fletcher chose to retire southwards and to reorganise.

In fact, *Shokaku* had not gone down. Once the fires on it had been brought under control the carrier was found not to be holed below the waterline, but even so, damage was severe and the ship needed shelter. When pilots returning from the strike against the US task force reported that both American carriers had been sunk, Takagi had no hesitation in detaching *Shokaku* at 1pm and ordering it back to Truk. After a perilous voyage during which the ship almost capsized in a gale, it eventually reached Japan and underwent lengthy repairs.

Although at this point Japanese jubilation at their imagined success against the Americans was very much misplaced, circumstances caused by human error now intervened to achieve what the enemy's air attacks had not. At 12.47pm, as Task Force Fox proceeded south, the *Lexington* was suddenly torn by a tremendous explosion amidships, well down in the bowels of the ship, which killed or disabled many damage control personnel and started numerous fires ·which were unfightable because of water mains severed by the blast. In his post-action report the *Lexington*'s commanding officer, Captain Frederick Sherman, remarked that at first the blast was thought to be due to a 'sleeper' (a bomb fitted with a delayed fuse) or a dud which suddenly went off. Later study, however, indicated the cause was to be found in the internal communications centre, where motor-generators had been left running when the room was evacuated due to fumes and malfunctioning ventilation. The motors were believed to have overheated, igniting a build-up of vapour from leaking aviation fuel pipelines which had been ruptured by the pounding endured by the ship when it was torpedoed.

In an interview given to the press a week later, Sherman (now promoted rear-admiral) recounted the events that followed:

> Simultaneously, ammunition stores started to explode, and the blaze spread to the hanger deck. All this time the engineering crew below deck had stuck to their post, although the intense heat was blistering the paint of the bulkheads around them. The rapidly-spreading fire, however, finally necessitated an order to the engineering men to come up on deck. Even as they came topside telephone communications failed. Had we delayed the order one minute none would have reached the top alive. As communications were destroyed and the stearing gear was gone, there was no chance of extinguishing the fire, and Rear-Admiral Fitch . . . decided to abandon ship. I gave the order at 5.7 p.m.
>
> At sunset, in orderly fashion, though reluctantly, the men were taken off by destroyers and cruisers. They were so calm that some went below deck and filled their helmets with ice cream from the ship's stores and went over the side eating it. All arranged their shoes in orderly rows before leaving. There were no casualties in the water. All resulted from combat.
>
> Admiral Fitch and I left the bridge together. I saw him off, then made a final inspection tour, and found 50 members of the gun crews who had not left yet. It was very touching when a petty-officer called for three cheers for the captain when they left. I then

slipped down the rope to the water, and was picked up and taken to a cruiser.

Sherman was taken to the heavy cruiser *Minneapolis*, where he reported to Fitch. With more than 90 per cent of *Lexington*'s complement recovered, all of the ship's company still living in fact, shortly before 8pm the destroyer USS *Phelps* fired five torpedoes at the wreck which was now ablaze along nearly its entire length; three of these hit, and the 'Lady Lex' went down in 2400 fathoms, taking the remains of 216 men killed during the day's action and 35 aircraft still on board. Sherman's post-action report contained a poignant commentary on the giant carrier's final moments:

> The picture of the burning and doomed ship was a magnificent but sad sight. The ship and crew had performed gloriously and it seemed too bad that she had to perish in her hour of victory. But she went to a glorious end, more fitting than the usual fate of the eventual scrap heap or succumbing to the perils of the sea. She went down in battle, after a glorious victory for our forces in which the *Lexington* and her air group played so conspicuous a part . . . As she went under a tremendous explosion occurred which rocked ships for miles around.

Although the loss of the *Lexington* was a severe blow to the Allies, the Japanese were in no frame of mind or position to take advantage of it. Takagi's losses had also been heavy. Quite apart from casualties among his aircrew, which included Takahashi, he had lost 45 of the 72 aircraft operational that morning. According to Okumiya, there was on board *Zuikaku* immediately after the battle only 24 fighters, nine torpedo-bombers and six dive-bombers still fit for further operations. (Against this Fitch had 37 attack planes and 12 fighters available.) With his fuel supplies running low, Takagi sought Inoue's permission to follow *Shokaku* out of the battle zone. The Japanese commander gave his approval, and at the same time cancelled the Moresby invasion operation completely.

According to Hiroyuki Agawa's account of events, officers of

Repeatedly torn by massive internal explosions and fiercely ablaze, the American carrier *Lexington* was clearly in its death throes when the surviving crew was ordered to abandon it shortly after 5pm on 8 May. Some 2700 men went hand-over-hand down lines over its sides to the water below, where they were picked up and taken to other ships of Task Force 17. (*AWM* neg.157901)

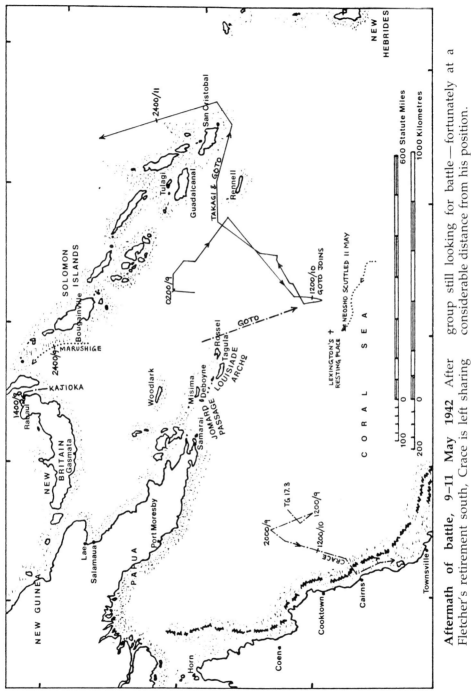

Aftermath of battle, 9–11 May 1942 After Fletcher's retirement south, Crace is left sharing the Coral Sea with Takagi's reduced striking group still looking for battle — fortunately at a considerable distance from his position.

Admiral Yamamoto's staff who had been monitoring proceedings from Combined Fleet Headquarters were incensed by Inoue's handling of the battle. Appalled by his conservative—even timid—leadership, many accused him of lack of fight or even of cowardice. When Yamamoto himself learnt that Inoue had allowed Takagi to withdraw, he was furious and issued countermanding orders at midnight requiring an immediate return to the Coral Sea to complete Fletcher's destruction. Takagi complied by turning south with his remaining force of *Zuikaku*, four cruisers and six destroyers.

Fletcher had not, in fact, regrouped for a return to the fray. The loss of the *Neosho* had removed the safe margin of available fuel oil for his ships, and in any event Nimitz ordered him to take his ships out of the Coral Sea area until Halsey's Task Force 16 reached him as a reinforcement. By noon on 10 May, when it was apparent that Fletcher's force was nowhere to be found and even Yamamoto had to admit that the American ships had left the area, Takagi's recall to Truk was sounded. The point at which he turned, almost due east of the *Lexington*'s resting place, would in fact become the furthest penetration south by Japanese surface ships during the war.

As a result of its movements during the night, Task Group 17.3 was well to the west when this major action between the two carrier groups took place. Having been sidelined throughout these momentous events, Crace knew nothing of them. He maintained his presence as a blocking force, remaining at action stations throughout the daylight hours in case his ships again were subjected to air attack. His expectation that Fletcher would take the trouble to keep him in the picture went unrealised, however, and consequently the action of 8 May could again only be followed from the confused radio communications monitored during the battle. These were mostly uninformative, though at times deeply moving to those on the bridge of the *Australia*. Recalls Mervyn Johnston, 'We could hear on the Voice Radio comments of various pilots... [who] in some cases were running out of fuel or could not land on the *Lexington* or the *Yorktown* as they were either damaged or on fire. Many messages were goodbyes to friends or loved ones.'

Dwindling fuel supplies in *Hobart* and the destroyers were beginning to reach worrying levels by this time. The force was being fairly continuously shadowed, however, with several sightings of mystery aircraft during the forenoon, and it seemed manifestly unsafe for fuelling to be undertaken. At 12.50 pm radar detected an approaching aircraft, and a few minutes later this plane came into view in the distance. It appeared to be an American B-17, but as it came into range of the ships the pilot failed to give the correct reply when challenged. The order was therefore given for the plane to be fired upon, causing it to speedily turn away again, an action which Crace later justified with the comment, 'I hope [it] will make him take the trouble to read his instructions.'

Shortly after this incident, the destroyer *Walke* experienced problems with the reduction gearing of one engine which left it able to manage just 13–14 knots maximum speed. *Perkins*, too, had problems, suffering a temporary stoppage through a loss of suction due to its low fuel level. Crace decided on some makeshift fuelling arrangements, instructing *Hobart* to transfer 200 tons to *Perkins* during the afternoon. He then detached the light cruiser after sunset under orders to accompany the stricken *Walke* to Townsville before itself going on to Brisbane. The next day the transfer of 300 tons of fuel from *Australia* to *Farragut* was carried out before noon. By these means Crace was able to maintain his presence as a blocking force in the area into 9 May, in the belief that Fletcher was still somewhere around and that this necessitated him maintaining position. In fact, Task Force 17 was already heading south out of the combat zone, leaving Crace's reduced squadron on its own. At this time, of course, Takagi's force was still in the Coral Sea hunting for Fletcher, though fortunately more than 700 miles away to the east.

By 7pm on 9 May Crace could only assume that Fletcher's carriers were also probably 'badly in need of replacement aircraft, bombs and torpedoes, while the destroyers of this Group were probably in need of fuel'. Although still without orders, or even information, he guessed that Fletcher had by now retired and contemplated doing the same. He was considerably irritated to hear BBC radio broadcasts declaring the battle over, asking himself, 'Where do they get this if I am kept in the dark?' He began to wonder whether, if this was just a lull, he should make a dash for Cid Harbour (the sheltered anchorage on the western shore of Whitsunday Island, 135 nautical miles south of Townsville, where the squadron's oiler *Kurumba* was waiting) and refuel in readiness for a resumption of operations. After much deliberation he decided to remain in the area until 1am on 10 May and, if no further information regarding enemy forces moving south had been received by this time, he would himself turn southward.

In accordance with this plan, the squadron reached the Great Barrier Reef before sunset on 10 May and entered the protected waters inside the Reef via the Grafton Passage. At 3.40pm that day Crace had sent off the flagship's Walrus with signals for Leary, asking what was going on and whether the object originally given to him still held. The opportunity was also taken to send off mail from the crew, with some relaxation of the normal censorship of letters. As Midshipman Smyth told his mother:

> A very hurried note, as we've suddenly been told that a mail will go in an hour's time. First I must reassure you in case the Jap claims over the wireless have frightened you — I'm still O.K. I'll try to give you an idea of what caused them to make that claim (i.e. that an Aust. cruiser of Canberra type (us) had been severely damaged) . . . We're allowed to say a bit about it for once, probably to help disprove the Japs' claim.

By noon the next day Cid Harbour was reached, and the ships began refuelling from the *Kurumba*. Earlier on the morning of his arrival, Crace received what he regarded as 'an extremely nice signal' from Fletcher detaching his squadron from Task Force 17. 'Sorry to leave you in precarious situation,' the message read, 'and congratulate you on your victory over bombers. Thank you for your unselfish and efficient co-operation.' The squadron's part in the Coral Sea battle was at an end, and it now reverted to its former identity as Task Force 44.

9 *Taking stock*

T HE wake of the Coral Sea action brought universal agreement that a major victory had been attained. But opinions differed over who had won it and at what cost, along with what had actually been at stake in the battle. Australian newspapers reported the terms of a rescript by Emperor Hirohito to Admiral Yamamoto, announced over Tokyo Radio on 12 May, expressing deep appreciation that an 'Anglo-American Fleet' had been 'heavily crushed' in the engagement. According to the summation of the battle's outcome by Imperial Headquarters, the Allied fleet had been effectively destroyed. Two US aircraft-carriers—one of the *Saratoga*-type and one of the *Yorktown* class—had been sunk, it was claimed, along with an American battle-ship of the *California*-type, a destroyer and a 20 000-ton tanker; 98 aircraft had been destroyed; and among the Allied naval units damaged were a British battleship of the *Warspite* class, a British cruiser of the *Canberra*-type, and an unidentified cruiser. Japanese losses were stated to be one small aircraft-carrier sunk and 31 planes missing. Though this assessment was not wilful embellishment, it was a significant over-estimation of the damage inflicted on Task Force 17 and Task Group 17.3 which was to have serious implications later.

For their part, Allied estimates of their success were no less inflated. As much as a month after the battle, official bulletins released to the press were still claiming that more than 15 Japanese ships had been sunk and more than 20 severely damaged during the Coral Sea engagement and the attack on Tulagi that preceded it. Sinkings allegedly included an aircraft-carrier, three heavy cruisers, one light cruiser, two destroyers, several transports and smaller ships, along with a cruiser and a destroyer also probably sunk, while the list of ships damaged embraced another carrier, three cruisers, two aircraft tenders and three destroyers. Despite the impression which might have formed in the minds of readers of these reports that a large proportion of the Japanese navy was now rusting on the ocean floor, the public was nonetheless advised that the Japanese remained numerically superior to Allied strength and retained the ability to attack again.

In all the publicity given to the battle and its consequences, real or imagined, there was never a doubt that Australia had been the direct target of the Japanese operation. The belief that the mainland itself had been, and was still, faced with the grim and dreaded threat of Japanese invasion was given expression at the highest national levels. Announcing in the federal parliament on 8 May that a great naval battle was then proceeding, Prime Minister John Curtin solemnly warned the nation:

> . . . events that are taking place to-day are of crucial importance to the whole conduct of the war in this theatre . . . I should add that at this moment nobody can tell what the result of the engagement may be. If it should go advantageously, we shall have cause for great gratitude and our position will then be somewhat clearer. But if we should not have the advantages from this battle for which we hope, all that confronts us is a sterner ordeal and a greater and grave responsibility. This battle will not decide the war; it will determine the immediate tactics which will be pursued by the Allied forces and by the common enemy.

The prime minister might have been understood from this to be talking of something less than actual invasion of the Australian mainland, although the leader of the United Australia Party on the opposition benches, Billy Hughes, that old warhorse who had led the nation in the First World War, believed he understood well enough what was meant when he added his voice to the rallying call that same night: 'To the ramparts then, Australians, and brace yourselves for the great struggle that looms darkly ahead.' Curtin, too, was clearer about what was on his mind when he said during a radio broadcast on the evening of 8 May: 'Invasion is a menace capable hourly of becoming an actuality.' Speaking in parliament again on 4 June, he expressed his belief that the events in the Coral Sea had been 'a signal success for the Allied forces engaged' which 'averted an immediate threat to Australian territory'.

Misapprehension on this scale about the actual object behind the Japanese moves in the Coral Sea battle might appear a little surprising, given the tremendous intelligence advantage enjoyed by the Allies through the American ability to read the enemy's naval code. It will be recalled, however, that this source had not revealed the destination of the troop transports known to be assembling in Rabaul harbour. So far as the Allied commanders knew, the enemy's southward thrust might very well mean nothing less than an imminent landing in Australia. The desperate military measures initiated to meet such an eventuality are graphically illustrated by a member of the Women's Auxiliary Australian Air Force working at a radar station at Lytton, at the mouth of the Brisbane River, who recalled the preparations for resistance which she discovered being taken as the Japanese troopships headed into the Coral Sea:

> Coming from duty one bright moonlit night, I noticed something strange about the shapes of some of the [mangrove] trees. It was 1 am, but seeing a light in the Commanding Officer's office, I knocked and asked, 'Sir, why is there a soldier sitting in the branches of every third tree, and facing out to sea?' He looked me in the eye and said, 'Corporal, there are no soldiers and if there are, you didn't see them. And if you saw them, you certainly will not mention them to anyone else!'

Such instances may seem ridiculous in hindsight, particularly in the secure knowledge that the Japanese plan did not, in fact, extend to a landing at Brisbane, or anywhere else on the Australian main-land. No-one could be sure of this at the time, however, and when a report was received on the afternoon of 9 May — the day after the carrier clash — that a large enemy force (including a carrier) was off Townsville, this grave news was taken at face value. Only after air strikes were launched against this target was the report found to be erroneous.

The conviction that Australia really was facing its darkest hour was firmly held in MacArthur's own headquarters. Responding to post-battle suggestions within the Australian government that Allied air forces under his command ought to have inflicted heavier losses on the Japanese than had actually been the case, MacArthur himself wrote to Curtin on 18 May to express his disappointment that there should be any criticism of what he considered to have been 'a very brilliant effort... which undoubtedly saved Australia from a definite and immediate threat'. The fact that the enemy did not seem to have suffered a particularly savage mauling only caused MacArthur's staff to be cautious in their predictions regard-ing likely developments. They could not believe that the enemy withdrawal on 8 May was more than a temporary respite while the invasion force regrouped, and they initially doubted that the engagement had even ended; on 9 May a communique was issued by the headquarters stating only that naval action in the Coral Sea had 'temporarily ceased'. The belief that the Japanese thrust would be renewed was widespread.

The continuing seriousness of the situation perceived to exist is evident from newspaper reports that Curtin had visited MacArthur's headquarters on 11 May to talk about 'preparations to meet any other sign of Japanese aggression'. These same reports stated that the Minister for the Army, Francis Forde, had also been conferring with General Sir Thomas Blamey, MacArthur's land force commander, about the Coral Sea action and its likely consequences, and 'the state of Australia's defences generally'. Forde was quoted in the *Sydney Morning Herald* as saying, 'Everything possible is being done to speed up the defences of Australia to meet any emergency', and the paper went on to announce:

> Studying maps and poring over experts' reports . . ., these civil and military leaders in the South-west Pacific were fully aware of the implications in this second phase of the struggle [following the Coral Sea]. Japan is capable of coming again, perhaps in greater force. Its losses in the Coral Sea were substantial, but by no means vital.

For the generation of Australians alive at the time, publicity surrounding the battle created a mystique which the passage of years and more accurate knowledge regarding the real Japanese purpose in May 1942 has still to fully erase. For many, the Battle of the Coral Sea remained 'the Battle that Saved Australia'. Despite the obvious exaggeration later apparent in such a title, the description still had a certain validity. A Japanese assault on Port Moresby, which almost certainly would have succeeded if it had been delivered, would have resulted in northern Queensland being subjected to heavy and sustained bombing. Also, had Moresby fallen quickly and cheaply in May, it is likely that Japanese strategy would have been revised to encompass the invasion option previously rejected. Indeed, a rethink of Japan's options must surely have occurred had Admiral Yamamoto secured the decisive victory over the US Pacific Fleet that he was seeking at Midway. Instead, the Battle of Midway fought on 4 June 1942 was a severe defeat for the Japanese Navy. Unaware that the Americans knew enough of his intentions to position three aircraft carriers (including the *Yorktown*, the damage sustained at the Coral Sea hastily repaired despite the Japanese belief that it had been sunk), and himself forced to leave two of his own best carrier units back in Japan (*Shokaku* undergoing repairs and *Zuikaku* still replacing planes and crews lost in the previous month's engagement), Yamamoto's planned knock-out blow was parried and returned. Taken by surprise, Admiral Nagumo's First Carrier Striking Force suffered the stunning loss of all four of its carriers.

Following the Midway upset, the Japanese postponed indefinitely any resumption of an advance towards the more distant objectives of the failed Operation 'MO' — that is, New Caledonia, Fiji and Samoa. A decision was taken to continue the attempt to capture Port Moresby but, having been denied the easy sea route, this advance would now be overland from the northern coast of New Guinea. Beginning in July, this new offensive would also, ultimately, be unsuccessful. Only belatedly, therefore, did it come to be realised by the Allies that the outcome of the Coral Sea battle, while entailing a heavier cost to themselves than the enemy, had actually been an significant strategic victory over the Japanese.

Meanwhile, important events had been taking place on board Crace's flagship in the wake of the Coral Sea. As soon as the squadron had reached its anchorage off Whitsunday Island on 11 May, Crace took the opportunity to have the commanding officers of *Chicago*, *Perkins* and *Farragut* join him at lunch for a 'wash-up' of the battle. This was principally to obtain their versions of precisely what had happened during the Coral Sea engagement for the purpose of compiling his official report. Joining them was Lieutenant-Commander Geoff Hall, an RAN officer from ACH Townsville, who flew down in *Australia*'s Walrus when the aircraft returned that morning from its previous day's mission of delivering signals and mail.

A number of important points and aspects were covered during these discussions, and Crace was delighted to hear that the squadron's fight with the Japanese torpedo-bombers had been recorded on movie film by a photographer on board *Chicago*. He was keen to obtain a copy of this footage for instructional purposes on *Australia*; but when he viewed a screening of it sometime later, he was disappointed to see how little of the air action had been actually captured on film. Interesting and useful though these discussions were, the real revelations of the day came from Hall. Not only did he bring the serious news regarding the loss of the *Lexington*, but after lunch he also informed Crace that US army bombers from Townsville had been involved in the attacks on his squadron during 7 May. As proof he produced photographs taken from the American planes during their bombing run. Crace was flabbergasted: 'It's almost incredible,' he spluttered into his diary.

After all his guests had left at about 4pm, Crace received a signal from Leary. This instructed him to send *Chicago* and *Perkins* to Sydney for a ten days' refit, and take the flagship and *Farragut* to Brisbane for further fuel and provisions prior to joining Halsey's Task Force 16. This group was still hastening south to link up with Fletcher and assist in ensuring that the Japanese naval forces withdrawn from the Coral Sea, having now dropped from sight, were not regrouping for a break-through between Fiji and the New Hebrides.

On the evening of 11 May *Chicago* and *Perkins* were accordingly detached to proceed to Sydney, and Crace also headed south, making for Brisbane. As he advised Royle, unless he received orders to the contrary he intended to put to sea just as soon as refuelling was completed and expected to link up with Task Force 16 about 18 May, after topping up with oil at Noumea. The next day, however, he received new orders from Halsey not to join him in the vicinity of Noumea but remain in the 'Sydney-Port Moresby area'. As there was no fuel available at ports north of Brisbane at this time, except for Townsville which could not accept ships larger than destroyers, Crace decided to continue on to Brisbane and await further developments there.

While still *en route* during 12 May, Crace spent most of the day working on his report and writing to his superiors in Melbourne. By now, his sense of disbelief at the news given to him the previous day was replaced by white-hot anger, and he gave vent to his outrage that, at the height of a critical sea action, his ships had been forced to dodge 'friendly' bombs as well as those of the enemy. He wrote, firstly, a fairly restrained letter of complaint to Leary which mentioned the bombing incident in relatively mild terms. His next letter, personally typed in the privacy of his cabin, was a lengthy and racy epistle to Royle. While he expected that Leary would pass on the letter he had just finished writing to him, there were, Crace said, 'some matters which I can't discuss with him' (Leary) which now prompted him to write to CNS separately.

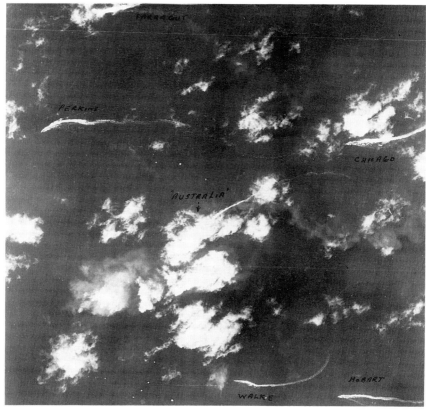

These two photographs in Crace's private papers were the proof positive that Task Group 17.3 had been bombed by US B-17s on 7 May. In the bottom photograph, HMAS *Australia* is directly beneath the bomb which has just been released. (*IWM negs.HU56168 & HU56169*)

Despite the fact that he had chosen to broach the subject with Leary, he still included plenty of forthright comment on the serious problem of aerial identification and reporting of ships. In his official report he was pointed in his references to the fact that 'aircraft from the US Army at Townsville' (referred to here as B-26s although the evidence remained that they were actually B-17s) had been 'good enough to photograph Task Group 17.3 a few seconds after "bombs release" thus proving beyond all doubt that they had attacked their own ships. Fortunately, their bombing, in comparison with that of the Japanese formation a few moments earlier, was disgraceful!' His private comments to Royle were, however, even blunter. Allied aircrews were, he considered, quite incapable of recognising their own ships, and he went on:

> In the High Level Bombing attack, the last three bombs to be dropped (and those which missed *Australia* by the greatest distance and nearly hit *Perkins*!) were dropped by three of our own B.17's which were actually above the Jap bombers. Can you beat it? They even took a photograph (which we have) to prove it! . . . Can nothing be done to train observers in the recognition of their own and enemy ships? Is the present inefficiency to be accepted and condoned? After all Australia hasn't got many ships and they are all very distinctive and the Japs should be easy enough to recognise. I should be very interested to hear what explanation the leader of the 3 B.17's had for bombing my force at a height from which no one could recognise a ship and for not seeing, recognising and attacking the 19 Jap bombers which were below them and could easily be seen from the surface at 14,000 feet. It is distressing to feel that we have to contend with the American air menace in addition to the Japanese and it is perhaps fortunate that the former are less efficient than the latter!!!!! Joking apart I would earnestly suggest that immediate steps be taken to institute regular and intensive training in the recognition of ships by all flying personnel of whatever nationality.

In addition to his acerbic observations on this score, he was also bitterly critical of the fact that throughout the battle he had been left totally in the dark as to what was happening. He made it clear to Royle that he did not blame Fletcher at all for this, 'both because he was otherwise very busily engaged and also because he naturally wished to keep W/T [radio] silence as far as possible'. But he considered there had been a lamentable failure on the part of other agencies, and he felt:

... most strongly that CWR [the Central War Room in Melbourne] could have taken a hand and let me know how the situation was developing ... The majority of stuff I got was enemy reports, generally incorrect, from aircraft direct or from ACH Townsville. These latter were later repeated word for word (and generally garbled) by COMSOUWESPAC. CWR appears merely to act as a rather indifferent Post Office and this is what I complained of before and was mildly rebuked ... I know very well how inefficient our aircraft reporting is but I should not have expected such a state of affairs to have been accepted as not capable of improvement.

Crace's restrained letter of complaint to Admiral Leary elicited soothing responses on both these matters in a reply dated 16 May. After offering his 'hearty congratulations' at the skilful hand-ling which avoided damage to Task Group 17.3 on 7 May, COMSOUWESPAC went on to remark:

I quite agree with you in your comments on the ineffective reconnaissance work done by our Army planes and we have taken up all the points raised in your letter with General Brett and I hope we can do better next time ... The trouble is that due to radio silence on the part of Fletcher we did not know any more about his movements than you did. In addition the fact that Army planes reported ships by wrong types and gave insufficient and often inaccurate reports made it hard for anyone here to see what was going on. However, as a result of your letter the whole system has been gone over and we hope to give you better service in the future. You can rest assured that we will do the best we can and don't hesitate to send in your criticisms as we know they are intended in the right spirit and we will try to correct them.

So far as the bombing incident was concerned, Leary reported that:

The Army is investigating ... and will do their best to prevent a recurrance [sic]. The trouble is, as with other matters, their pilots are civilians who have had three months training at an airport and are then sent out here and have to be intrusted [sic] with important missions for which they are in no sense qualified — but it is all they have. They are taking steps to try to improve their training at every opportunity and I gave them extracts from your letter which has had a very beneficial effect.

In fact, the outcome to this latter issue was not as satisfactory as Leary's letter suggested. Far from admitting the mistaken attack on Crace's squadron, Lieutenant-General George Brett, MacArthur's air commander, flatly denied on 19 May that there had ever been any such incident and refused further discussion. There was no doubt whatever that Brett was wrong. Even the official history of the US Army Air Force reported admissions by 19th Bombardment Group officers that Allied naval units had been attacked during the Coral Sea battle.

Records of Allied Air Forces Headquarters show that on 7 May two missions were flown by flights of three B-17s from the 19th Group in North Queensland against shipping in the area of the Jomard Passage. During both missions, attacks were delivered in the designated area although the time and coordinates of these is not listed. This imprecision was conceivably due to 'drastic measures' alleged by Australian historian Gavin Long to have been taken to expunge all references to the affair from the historical record, although proof that such occurred has yet to emerge. If a deliberate cover-up was attempted, however, it was certainly not very thorough.

Apart from the photographic proof which remained to refute the position adopted by General Brett, there was an implicit admission in the files of Allied Air Forces Headquarters that some incident of the sort might have happened. In a report dated 29 May, Air Commodore Frank Lukis, the RAAF officer commanding North Eastern Area of Australia's air defence organisation, stated: 'Perhaps the outstanding lesson in the Coral Sea engagement is the great difficulty experienced by the American Bombardment crews in distinguishing friend from foe on the high seas when such are almost in contact.' After discussing the sort of measures necessary to overcome the problem, Lukis went on to say: 'It is appreciated that there are objections to this system, but some means must be found to enable bombardment aircraft to be able to differentiate between friend and foe, because this is impossible by visual means from the bombing height.'

More explicit was an remarkable account published in at least one Australian newspaper which, although somewhat misleading in its contents, is still recognisable as a description of the accidental bombing of Crace's squadron by the aircrew which carried out the attack! The Melbourne *Argus* reported that Captain Harry Speih, of Portland, Oregon, had led a formation of long-range land-based bombers 'which sighted warships twisting and turning to escape heavy attacks from 15 Japanese bombers on the 2nd day of the battle', and went on to quote his version of events:

We thought they were our Navy bombers attacking Japanese
warships . . . and we were preparing to lend them a hand when
we found they were Japanese bombers, and the warships were
ours, so we kept fairly high and cruised around watching the
fight. One Australian cruiser was taking everything the Nips had,
weaving in and out among the bomb bursts so neatly that you
would think she knew where they were going to fall. One salvo
fell right around her, and it looked like the end, but she rode out
of a smother of foam just the same as ever. It was a grand bit of
seamanship. The Japs just could not hit any of them.

While omitting to mention that Captain Speih's planes *did* join in
'lending the Japanese a hand' before they realised their mistake,
here was a description which admitted the presence of army
bombers at the site of the incident about which Crace had complained.

As one biographer of MacArthur has observed, no evidence has
been uncovered indicating the supreme commander's opinion of
or intervention in the affair, 'but the shameful matter undoubtedly
did not improve his regard for either Brett or Leary. Fortunately for
relations between MacArthur and Nimitz, the episode did not
involve Fletcher's ships.' In Brett's case, it can be surmised that the
incident added to MacArthur's dissatisfaction with his air commander, and contributed to Brett's replacement within a few
months for 'error[s] in judgement'.

For Crace's part, there is no suggestion that he harboured any
special animus towards his US colleagues, despite his blunt talking
to Royle. This is evident from the tribute later paid to him by the
American commander of his destroyer screen during 'Crace's
Chase': in the words of Commander Francis McInerney, the
admiral had shown himself to be an 'excellent seaman' and also a
'gallant gentleman who accepted the United States ships into his
command with warmth, affection and admiration for their efficiency'.

Within days of Crace's arrival at Brisbane from Cid Harbour on
13 May, he found the sense of high expectancy following the action
in the Coral Sea ebbing away. By 17 May it was clear that the
Japanese would not be immediately resuming major operations to
Australia's north, and both Fletcher's Task Force 17 and Halsey's
Task Force 16 were withdrawn to Hawaii—in time, as it turned
out, for the forthcoming clash around Midway. This left Task Force

44 once more on its own in providing Australia's naval defence.

During the rest of May, the composition of Crace's squadron underwent numerous changes. Awaiting the arrival of the flagship and *Farragut* at Brisbane were *Hobart* and *Walke*, but the latter was refitting and did not rejoin Crace's flag, and *Farragut* was detached from the Task Force at this point. Over the next few weeks, however, six more American ships arrived to join the squadron, these being the cruiser *Salt Lake City* and destroyers *Henley, Helm, Flusser, Mugford* and *Bagley*.

While still berthed at Brisbane Crace experienced a second startling example of the poor ship-recognition abilities of US army aircrews. As later recounted by Commander Galfry Gatacre, who had joined the flagship on 17 May as the new Staff Officer (Operations and Intelligence), a reconaissance report was received of an enemy aircraft carrier off the Queensland coast. Further reports stated that the carrier had turned into the wind and was operating aircraft. Crace discussed the reports with Farncomb and Gatacre, and all agreed 'that it would reduce the threats to the city, and that our ships (Task Force 44) would be better off in a defensive formation in Moreton Bay, rather than alongside wharves in the Brisbane River'. Emergency preparations were initiated to proceed down the river when a message was received, from the same aircraft, cancelling previous reports and stating that what he had been watching and reporting was not an aircraft carrier but a reef awash. Wrote Gatacre: 'A reef awash turning into the wind and operating aircraft? Some reef!'

During this period, too, Crace asked Navy Office if he could take *Australia* down to Sydney to have the flagship fitted with radar but was apparently refused. At this time *Canberra, Chicago* and *Perkins* were all refitting in Sydney; they were still there when three Japanese midget submarines penetrated the harbour on the night of 31 May-1 June, bent on sinking as many major Allied warships as possible; *Chicago* escaped damage when torpedoes fired at it missed their mark and struck a converted ferry being used to house naval ratings. It was only on 1 June, when the bulk of the Task Force proceeded into Moreton Bay for exercises, that these three ships left Sydney and came north. By 4 June the whole of Task Force 44 was together at sea, an assembly of strength which was short-lived. That same day Crace transferred his flag to *Canberra* from *Australia*, which then departed for Sydney with *Helm*, before the Task Force returned to Brisbane the following day.

HMAS *Australia* (in foreground) shown with HMAS *Hobart* shortly after the Coral Sea battle. The 'dazzle' camouflage in which both cruisers fought the battle has now been replaced by dark blue or flat grey paintwork such as that worn by ships of the U.S. Navy. (*RAN Photographic Unit*)

On 6 June, with *Chicago* now back with his flag, Crace renewed contact with Captain Bode, whom he had found 'a really first class chap with very sound views'. This was the opinion Crace had expressed to Royle in his blunt letter of 12 May, and he now found that Bode was carrying various replies to this particular letter to give to him. He was somewhat amazed and embarrassed to learn from Bode that Royle had actually passed the letter across to Leary, and plainly regretted the candour with which he had written to his RN superior. As he noted in his diary, the letter was 'extremely outspoken and I had said [I] was writing to him as there was one or two matters I didn't like to mention to Leary. It just shows that one can't trust people & it is very unwise to write unguardedly.' There was, however, little worry that this episode would complicate his relations with Leary, as Crace was aware that his days as Task Force commander were numbered in any event.

From the time the squadron had reached Cid Harbour after the Coral Sea action, Crace had been dwelling on his replacement Crutchley's arrival as he was keen to be off and wanted no delays. Finding that news of his imminent relief was all over the flagship due to a leak that he could not trace, he urged Royle in his letter of 12 May that Crutchley should come to Brisbane to assume the command as soon as he arrived, as opportunities for joining the squadron might subsequently prove to be scarce, and that in any event the changeover should not be protracted:

> It certainly will not help him to get into the picture and will be an embarrassment to us both. I shall try to make notes of all matters of interest which we can discuss briefly and I consider that more than a day together is unnecessary and undesirable. You may be quite sure that I will not go until Crutchley is satisfied but I know that if I was in his place I should hate to have my predecessor lurking about.

Finally, on 12 June, Crutchley arrived in Brisbane by train to effect the transfer of command. At 8am the next morning Crutchley's flag was broken in *Hobart*, and at 5pm that same day Crace's flag was struck in *Canberra*. On 14 June Crace flew out of Brisbane bound for Sydney, and Crutchley transferred his flag to *Canberra* on his formal assumption of command of Task Force 44 at 8am that day. For Crace there was the significance that he had ended his term as RACAS, as he began it, with the cruiser bearing the name of his home town as his flagship.

The next few days were spent by Crace making farewell rounds in Sydney and in Melbourne. Although impatient to be on his way back to England, he did not obtain passage on a ship for several weeks. On 2 July he sailed with his wife Carola and son Nicholas aboard the troopship *Wahine* bound for Auckland, where a local newspaper quoted him as saying that the Coral Sea battle had been an 'absolutely grand farewell to me from Australian waters'. Onward passage to England, via the Panama Canal and the Canadian port of Halifax, was obtained in the passenger ship *Capetown Castle* on 15 July. The voyage through the Caribbean was at a time when German submarine activity was at a peak, but the Craces' ship got through unscathed after picking up two boatloads of survivors from sinkings.

Their joy at having safely reached English soil, disembarking at bomb-ravaged Liverpool on 20 August, was dampened to a degree by the announcement which met them regarding the loss of HMAS *Canberra* off Savo Island, at Guadalcanal, on 9 August. *Chicago* was also damaged in this fight, one of four American cruisers made casualties in a daring Japanese night action. Crace had written to Bode shortly before his departure, receiving a reply dated 7 July which was a heartfelt tribute to the warm relations they enjoyed. Bode had written:

My dear Admiral,
You could not possibly imagine my joy, happiness and the sense of durable satisfaction I experienced when I opened your delightful memento, read the inscription on it together with your characteristically gracious note.

I shall treasure both always, just as you are permanently enshrined in our hearts and affections as a man, an officer and a gentleman, by whose example we have all profited so happily and so immeasurably.

I cherish the hope that the boomerang symbolizes a reunion when we shall have successfully concluded the various tasks in which we are so unitedly, and with such singleness of purpose, engaged.

In the meantime be assured that my thoughts and good wishes will follow you always as do, more immediately, my hopes that you and Mrs. Crace and Nicholas will have a safe, and not too uncomfortable, journey home.

With abiding esteem and affectionate regard, believe me, as always, sincerely.

Howard Bode

Bode survived the Guadalcanal disaster, unlike Captain Frank Getting who perished with *Canberra*, but sadly he did not see out the war. Posted in 1943 to command the naval station at Balboa, in the US Canal Zone at Panama, he died on 20 April 1943 as a non-war casualty.

After a month's leave, Crace took up his new appointment as Admiral Superintendent of the Chatham dockyard in Kent, south-east of London, on 15 October 1942. This proved to be also his final active appointment in the navy, as he was advised a month earlier that he would be placed on the retired list and promoted vice-admiral as soon as an officer junior to him on the gradation list achieved that rank. His transfer to the retired list occurred on 29 October that year but, although now officially retired, he continued in his appointment for the remainder of the war. A final highlight of the year 1942 was the award of the Distinguished Service Cross to son Allan for gallantry while serving as gunnery control officer of HMS *Quentin* the day before this destroyer was sunk by torpedo-bombers off Bone, in the western Mediterranean, on 2 December; survivors from the *Quentin* were taken to Bone by HMAS *Quiberon*.

Until closed down in 1984, Chatham was one of the oldest dockyards in England and had long been an important centre for the construction and repair of naval ships. Although building some of the most powerful ships in the world in the late nineteenth century, the yard had been unable to handle the new Dreadnought class of battleships in the early twentieth century and turned to specialising in submarine construction. It was in this role that the dockyard was operating when Crace arrived, and during the years he remained there six submarines and two sloops were launched or laid down in the yard, and hundreds of other ships repaired and refitted.

Crace thoroughly enjoyed the life at Chatham. It was strange, he later noted, that although Chatham was closer to Germany and in a more direct line to London than any of the three main British dockyards, it hardly suffered at all from enemy bombing—'not withstanding the fact that all raids on London both by bombs and doodlebugs passed over it'. He took more than a purely professional interest in the facility in his charge, and on his departure left a compilation entitled 'Some Notes on the History of Chatham Dockyard' which provided a detailed chronology of the place; listed under the authorship of 'J. G. Grace' [sic], this was foremost among secondary sources used extensively in writing the history of the dockyard 35 years later.

Crace remained at Chatham until July 1946, having been promoted on the retired list to the rank of admiral in September of the previous year. In the New Year's honours list of 1947 he was created a Knight Commander of the Order of the British Empire (KBE) in recognition of his war services. His last activity in uniform was to head a technical committee formed to advise the government of newly-independent India on the reorganisation and improvement of the naval dockyard at Bombay. After three months spent in Bombay, the committee prepared its findings and Crace delivered a copy of the finished report to the commander-in-chief of the Royal Indian Navy during a visit to Delhi on 25 March 1947. Two months later he received a letter from the Admiralty conveying the appreciation of the Indian government for his work. The Indian government was 'greatly impressed by the very lucid, comprehensive and helpful report . . ., which was produced as expeditiously by the Committee under your Chairmanship'. Crace took considerable satisfaction in this task, commenting later that 'my committee was an ideal one as it consisted of one other member beside myself with a secretary'.

In retirement Crace returned to live at his home at Hawkley, then a village of 200 inhabitants. It was a big house with a big garden which eventually became too much for him and his wife. Around 1952 they moved to Longacre, a smaller and more convenient house three kilometres away in Liss, a commuter town of about 3500 people. He lived a quiet existence, pursuing his hobby of bookbinding which he had begun for relaxation when commanding the Australian Squadron during the war.

Not unnaturally, he remained keenly interested in any discussion or public mention of the Coral Sea battle. His private papers, deposited with the Imperial War Museum in London by his widow, bear testimony to the care with which he assembled and maintained his wartime diaries and other records in his possession, having no doubt of their historical significance. When consulted in 1957 in connection with the writing of the British official war history, he expressed personal views regarding the conduct of the battle which would place him at variance with judgements expressed by the US Navy official historian, Samuel Morison, ten years later.

Fletcher comes in for some sharp criticism in the US account over the wisdom of the tactical decision which had produced 'Crace's Chase' on 7 May 1942, commenting that:

> Fletcher later explained that he had detached Crace because he expected an air duel with enemy carriers, and wished to ensure that the Japanese invasion should be thwarted, even if they finished him. But, if Takagi had stopped Fletcher, Crace's ships would probably have been chewed up too; and, by sending Crace chasing westward, Fletcher weakened his already exiguous anti-aircraft screen and lessened his chances of checking Takagi. Conversely, if Fletcher won the carrier battle he would be in a position to break up the Port Moresby Invasion Group even if they did turn the corner. Possibly this diversion served the good purpose of puzzling the enemy and causing him to concentrate his land-based air on Crace's cruisers instead of Fletcher's carriers; but it was only by a special dispensation of Providence that the Support Group escaped a fatal bombing.

Crace did not agree that Fletcher had been wrong in the decision he had made. Asked about this very point by a member of the Admiralty's Historical Section, he had replied in November 1957 that he felt the commander of Task Force 17 had been justified in detaching him because the 'advantage to be gained by possibly catching the Moresby Invasion Group in the Jomard Passage far outweighed that gained by increasing the Anti-Aircraft screen by the ships of my Force'.

Possibly Crace's understanding attitude towards the perilous position in which he had been placed by Fletcher's actions 15 years earlier was influenced by a feeling of regard for Fletcher personally. In early June 1942, while preparing to wind up his command as RACAS, he had received a letter from Commander William Adams RN, captain of HMAS *Kanimbla*, who had written to convey a message which Fletcher had asked should be passed to him. Fletcher wanted Crace to know that when he detached Task Group 17.3 towards the Jomard Passage it had been his intention to follow and give air support to the group, but that due to the situation which developed during the morning he was unable to carry out this intention. 'He feels that he left you badly in the lurch,' Adams reported, 'and as I have said, was very anxious that you should understand the position.'

It remains unknown what Crace thought of other of Morison's later judgements. Perhaps modesty inhibited him from having anything to say about the importance of the part his squadron had been called on to play during the battle. The American official historian had characterised 'Crace's Chase' as having 'served no useful purpose', although he allowed that it had at least been notable for having proved that 'ships of two nations could be made into an excellent tactical unit', and that the task group's escape from loss on 7 May had been 'a tribute to its training, and to the high tactical competence of its commander'. Certainly Task Group 17.3 had seen only a brief moment of action which stood apart from the great clash between the carriers. Yet the ferocity of the air attack endured by Crace's ships should not be trivialised. They had come under air attack as heavy as that which sank the British capital ships *Prince of Wales* and *Repulse* in December 1941; it was, as several historians have recognised, only the fact that the RAN had learnt a lot in the subsequent few months which enabled Crace's ships to escape without suffering any hits. Moreover Crace's role was actually directly concerned with the primary aim of the action—not guarding against a mythical invasion of Australia, but turning back the Japanese expeditionary force on its way to capture Port Moresby. Although doubt remains whether it was the sighting of Crace's squadron barring the way of the Japanese convoy or the sighting of Fletcher's carriers, or both, that caused Admiral Inoue to turn the convoy away, there can be no question that the enemy commander was forced to take account of the presence of *both* forces. Crace had therefore been an important element in shaping the way matters had developed on 7 May, which was when the primary movement towards Moresby had been stopped.

It remains, too, to be wondered what Crace thought of the attention accorded to the battle within Australia over subsequent years. He was certainly aware of the visits made to Australia by US ships and naval figures during annual Coral Sea celebrations organised by the Australian-American Association; among Crace's papers is the text of an address given over the Australian Broadcasting Commission in May 1967 by Admiral David L. McDonald,

---

Admiral A. W. Radford, the chief US guest at the 1955 Coral Sea anniversary celebrations, takes the salute at the march in Melbourne. The uniformed officers to his left are Lieutenant-General Sir Sydney Rowell (former CGS) and Vice-Admiral Sir John Collins (CNS). Despite his role in the battle, Crace was never invited to take part in these annual commemorations in Australia. (*AWM neg.44321*)

the US Navy's Chief of Naval Operations and guest of honour at that year's ceremonies. It was fair to say that, despite his just claims to a share of the spotlight on such an occasion, there was apparently little thought given by organisers of Coral Sea commemorations to the 'home-grown' product.

The neglectful attitude of Australians to the part played by their own naval forces in the battle was a point noted by historian Malcolm Ellis, writing under the pseudonym 'Ek Dum', in the *Bulletin* magazine during May 1954. Commenting on the presence in Australia of Admiral Halsey, 'whom Australians are delighted to honor, along with the US carrier *Tarawa* and her escort *O'Bannion*, in the current celebrations', Ellis referred to Fletcher and Crace as the 'honored ones' deserving of recognition specifically for the Coral Sea engagement. He went on to observe:

> Amid the celebration nobody seems to have thought of a solemn national ceremony to mark the part of H.M.A.S. *Australia*, now in her home-base of Sydney going through the final period of her last commission, the leader of the Australian squadron in the Coral Sea operations . . . There should be some national good-bye to her, some permanent memorial to her as the senior representative surviving of World War II's grandest little naval force of any nation, and the furthest ranging, which makes this country's name a proud thing to hear wherever fighting seamen gather.

Decommissioned later that year, *Australia* was sold for scrapping in England in January 1955. On leaving Sydney for the last time on 26 March, it was afforded a mighty farewell by hundreds of small craft which escorted it to the harbour heads. It was a scene reminiscent of that witnessed by Crace 30 years earlier when the first *Australia* went to meet its end.

After a seven-year battle with leukaemia, Crace died at his home on 11 May 1968, aged 81. At St Mary's Church, Liss, a week later, a memorial service held for him was attended by no fewer than ten admirals. There was, however, no representative of the Royal Australian Navy, nor of Australia as a whole, to honour a commander and a fellow countryman who played a leading role at the forefront of the nation's defence during a heroic moment in its history.

Bibliography

Crace Papers
E. K. Crace, papers (MS 1177) and letterbook (microfilm G6622) in NLA, and photo album in possession of Mr E. J. L. Crace of Cobbitty, NSW
Admiral Sir J. G. Crace, papers, diaries and photo albums (4 boxes: 69/18/ 1–4) in IWM, and papers and photo album in possession of Rev. J. A. Crace of Petersfield, Hants, Eng

Personal Communications
Mr E. J. L. Crace
Rev. J. A. Crace
Mr N. K. Crace of Overton, Hants, Eng
Commodore A. N. Dollard of Mosman, NSW
Mr C. Hemming of Ryde, NSW
Mrs F. L. Humphries of Bondi Beach, NSW
Mr T. M. Johnston of Fairfield, NSW
Mr J. B. Langrell of Strathfield, NSW
Lieutenant-Commander R. F. Moag of Sans Souci, NSW
Vice-Admiral Sir Richard Peek of Monaro Highway, via Cooma, NSW
Captain R. C. Savage of Mosman, NSW
Mr R. E. Scrivener of Forestville, NSW
Commodore D. H. D. Smyth of Toorak, Vic
Mr Frank J. Westley of Silver City, New Mexico, USA
Mr Edward J. Znosko of Riverside, Rhode Island, USA

Unpublished Sources
Coral Sea battle files and J. G. Crace biographical file, in Naval Historical Section, Department of Defence, Canb
AWM 69, item 23/74 (Anzac Squadron, TF 44, TF 74), AWM 78, HMAS *Hobart*: war diary Nov. 1940-Sep. 1943, and reports of proceedings Jun. 1941-Sep. 1942
Australian Archives (ACT), AA1969/100/6, item 373/25A (shore-based aircraft during Coral Sea)
Australian Archives (Vic), MP 1587, item 123V (Riley murder), MP 691,

item 4011/26/1 (Gordon and Elias), MT 1214, item 445/201/230 (Gordon and Elias)

NSW Department of Corrective Services: sentence and description records (Gordon and Elias)

Official Printed Sources

Commonwealth Parliamentary Debates, vol.170: 1060–61; vol.171: 2183 *Navy List* Lond: HMSO (various years)

Published Works

Agawa, H. (1979) *The Reluctant Admiral: Yamamoto and the Imperial Navy,* Tokyo: Kodansha International

Bradford, E. (1959) *The Mighty Hood,* Lond: Hodder & Stoughton

Coles, A. and Briggs E. (1985) *Flagship Hood,* Lond: Robert Hale

Detwiler, D. S. and Burdick C. B. (1980) *War in Asia and the Pacific,* vols.5, 7, New York: Garland

Fitzgerald, A. J. (1987) *Canberra in Two Centuries: A Pictorial History,* Canb: Clareville Press

Gatacre, G. G. O. (1982) *Reports of Proceedings,* Syd: Nautical Press

Gill, G. H. (1957) *Royal Australian Navy 1939–1942,* Canb: AWM

———— (1968) *Royal Australian Navy 1942–1945,* Canb: AWM

Gillett, R. and Graham C. (1977) *Warships of Australia,* Adel: Rigby

Gillison, D. N. (1962) *Royal Australian Air Force 1939–1942,* Canb: AWM

Harker, J. S. (1980) *HMNZS Achilles,* Auckland: William Collins

Hough, R. (1986) *The Longest Battle: The War at Sea 1939–45,* New York: William Morrow

Hoyt, E. P. (1970) *How They Won the War in the Pacific,* New York: Weybright and Talley

Humble, R. (1982) *Aircraft Carriers: The Illustrated History,* Hadley Wood, Eng: Winchmore Publishing

Humphries, F. L. 'The Craces of Gungahleen', *Canberra and District Historical Society Journal,* Dec. 1968

James, D. C. (1975) *The Years of MacArthur,* vol.2, Boston: Houghton Mifflin

Johnston, S. (1942) *Queen of the Flat-Tops,* New York: E. P. Dutton

Karig, W. & Kelley W. (1944) *Battle Report: Pearl Harbour to Coral Sea,* New York: Farrar & Rinehart

TKS (1981) *The King's School Register,* Parramatta, NSW: Council of TKS

———— *The King's School Magazine,* Sep. 1919, 1116, May 1940, 39, Aug. 1971, 11

Kinnane, G. (1989) *George Johnston: A biography,* Ringwood, Vic: Penguin

Kirby, S. W. (1958) *The War Against Japan,* vol.2, Lond: HMSO

Lind, L. J. & Payne, M. A. (1971) *H.M.A.S. Hobart: The Story of the 6 inch Cruiser 1938–1962,* Syd: NHSA

Long, G. M. (1969) *MacArthur as Military Commander,* Lond: B. T. Batsford

MacDougall, P. (1981) *The Chatham Dockyard Story,* Rochester, Eng: Rochester Press

McGuire, F. M. (1948) *The Royal Australian Navy: Its Origins, Development and Organization*, Melb: Oxford University Press

Macintyre, D. (1966) *The Battle for the Pacific*, Lond: B. T. Batsford

Millot, B. A. (1974) *The Battle of the Coral Sea*, London: Ian Allan

Montgomery, M. (1981) *Who Sank the Sydney?*, North Ryde, NSW: Cassell

Morison, S. E. (1965) *The Rising Sun in the Pacific: 1931-April 1942*, Boston: Little, Brown & Co.

―――― (1967) *Coral Sea, Midway and Submarine Actions: May 1942-August 1942*, Boston: Little, Brown & Co.

Okumiya, M. & Horikoshi, J. (1957) *Zero!: The Story of the Japanese Navy Air Force 1937–1945*, Lond: Cassell

Payne, M. A. (1973) *H.M.A.S. Canberra*, Syd: NHSA

―――― (1975) *H.M.A.S. Australia: The story of the 8 inch Cruiser 1928–1955*, Syd: NHSA

―――― (1978) *H.M.A.S. Perth: The Story of the 6 inch Cruiser 1936–1942*, Syd: NHSA

Potter, E. B. (1976) *Nimitz*, Annapolis: Naval Institute Press

―――― (1985) *Bull Halsey*, Annapolis: Naval Institute Press

Prange, G. W. (with D. M. Goldstein and K. V. Dillon) (1982) *Miracle at Midway*, New York: McGraw-Hill

Preston, A. (1979) *Aircraft Carriers*, Lond: Bison

Roberts, J. A. (1982) *The Battlecruiser Hood*, Annapolis: Naval Institute Press

Robertson, J. R. (1981) *Australia at War 1939–1945*, Melb: Heinemann

Waters, S. D. (1956) *The Royal New Zealand Navy*, Wellington: Department of Internal Affairs

Stevenson, C. G. & Darling, H. (eds.) (1984) *The WAAAF Book*, Sydney: Hale & Iremonger

Winter, B. (1984) *H.M.A.S. Sydney: Fact, Fantasy and Fraud*, Brisbane: Boolarong Publications

Zammit, A. 'Rear Admiral Farncomb' *Naval Historical Review*, Sep. 1988.

Newspapers

Age (Melb) 31 Oct. 1939

Argus (Melb) 2, 3, 24, 30, 31 Oct., 14 Nov. 1939, 22, 26 Jun. 1942

Bulletin (Syd) 23 Apr. 1941, 5 May 1954

Canberra Times 7 Oct. 1926, 31 Jan. 1928

Daily Telegraph (Syd) 22 Feb. 1940

Queanbeyan Observer (NSW) 20 Oct. 1899

Sydney Morning Herald 14 Apr. 1924, 1 Oct. 1926, 31 Jan. 1928, 4 Oct., 2, 14 Nov. 1939, 12, 22 Feb., 2 Apr. 1940, 3 Jul. 1941, 28 Apr., 1, 9, 11, 12, 13 May, 13, 15 Jun., 9 Jul. 1942, 17 May 1968

The Times (Lond) 1 July 1941, 1 Jan. 1947, 13, 20 May 1968

West Australian (Perth) 17 Mar. 1941

Index